Designing a
Concept-Based
Curriculum
for English Language Arts

In memory of my parents.

Lois A. Lanning

Foreword by H. LYNN ERICKSON

Designing a
Concept-Based
Curriculum
for English Language Arts

MEETING THE **COMMON CORE**
WITH INTELLECTUAL INTEGRITY, K–12

CORWIN
A SAGE Company

CORWIN
A SAGE Company

FOR INFORMATION:

Corwin
A SAGE Company
2455 Teller Road
Thousand Oaks, California 91320
(800) 233-9936
www.corwin.com

SAGE Publications Ltd.
1 Oliver's Yard
55 City Road
London EC1Y 1SP
United Kingdom

SAGE Publications India Pvt. Ltd.
B 1/I 1 Mohan Cooperative Industrial Area
Mathura Road, New Delhi 110 044
India

SAGE Publications Asia-Pacific Pte. Ltd.
3 Church Street
#10-04 Samsung Hub
Singapore 049483

Publisher: Lisa Luedeke
Acquisitions Editor: Carol Chambers Collins
Associate Editor: Megan Bedell
Editorial Assistant: Sarah Bartlett
Production Editor: Cassandra Margaret Seibel
Copy Editor: Melinda Masson
Typesetter: C&M Digitals (P) Ltd.
Proofreader: Annie Lubinsky
Indexer: Kathy Paparchontis
Cover Designer: Michael Dubowe
Permissions Editor: Adele Hutchinson

Copyright © 2013 by Corwin

Printed in the United States of America.

Library of Congress Cataloging-in-Publication Data

Lanning, Lois A.
Designing a concept-based curriculum for English language arts: meeting the common core with intellectual integrity, K–12/Lois A. Lanning.

pages cm
Includes bibliographical references and index.

ISBN 978-1-4522-4197-5 (pbk.: alk. paper)

1. Language arts (Elementary)—Curricula—United States—States. 2. Language arts (Elementary)—Standards—United States—States. 3. Language arts (Secondary)—Curricula—United States—States. 4. Language arts (Secondary)—Standards—United States—States. I. Title.

LB1576.L338 2013
372.6—dc23   2012037719

This book is printed on acid-free paper.

15 16 17 18 19 10 9 8 7 6 5 4 3 2

Contents

Additional materials and resources related to *Designing a Concept-Based Curriculum for English Language Arts* can be found at www.corwin.com/conceptbasedcurriculumK-12.

Foreword

If you are a teacher, a principal, a curriculum leader, or an instructional coach, you are in for an educator's treat.

Lois Lanning's book, *Designing a Concept-Based Curriculum for English Language Arts,* is the most forward-thinking, cutting-edge treatment for the design of curriculum and instruction in this area on the market today. Here are the three major reasons that I say this:

1. Most books for English language arts instruction focus on teaching the "themes" of books as the first priority; the development of processes, skills, and instructional strategies seems to take a back seat.

2. Teachers want to use diverse materials, both fiction and nonfiction, in working with their students, but district curriculum too often mandates a particular text or list of texts that must be used for particular units of study.

3. English language arts curriculum generally continues to be driven by book titles and skill objectives that fail to reach deeper, conceptual understanding and the ability to transfer knowledge.

Lois alleviates these problems with a step-by-step description of how to design *concept-based* English language arts units that teach far more than the themes of individual works of fiction. Teachers learn how to design units that focus on developing an understanding of the conceptual ideas in content, processes, strategies, and skills so that students can transfer their learning across multiple types of literary material and genres. The materials are not the end point of instruction—they are the tools for developing deeper conceptual understandings of the *why*—why teach and learn these processes, skills, and strategies as they are employed across a diverse selection of text material?

When curricula are not concept-based, we tend to "cover" content and skill objectives mindlessly—checking off verbs and topics, or skills, with the satisfaction of knowing that we are "getting through the curriculum." But there is a major problem with this outdated model—we "assume" that students have conceptual understanding of what they are learning. Four decades of experience have shown me clearly that we cannot make this assumption. If we want students to retain what they learn, and be able to transfer that knowledge to new situations, we must teach them to understand the relationships between the facts and processes and the conceptual levels of knowledge and understanding. We must provide instruction that builds an understanding of the overarching generalization or principle represented by a task. Students need to develop the conceptual language of the disciplines as they progress through school if they are to cogently explain their understandings. *Designing a Concept-Based Curriculum for English Language Arts* not only shows teachers a detailed plan for designing language arts units that support teaching beyond lists of discrete and disconnected skills, but is a book that explains clearly why curriculum and instruction must make this shift from assuming understanding to teaching *for* understanding.

One of the greatest thrills for a teacher is when a student goes on to become a teacher because of his or her impact during the student's early education. I feel like that thrilled teacher when I see how Lois took my teaching and extended it, creating her own teaching, into her strong area of expertise in English language arts. Lois participated in one of my workshops 17 years ago. She came up to me at the end of the workshop, and I could tell she had that "fire in her belly" for concept-based curriculum and instruction. That workshop led to a working relationship and friendship that has continued to this day. If you have a colleague in your life with whom you can share a complex idea, and he or she is able to extend your thoughts without so much as even having a detailed explanation, you know what I mean.

I have a confession to make here. When I first met Lois, I did not think that processes had "concepts." In fact, I think I even wrote in one of my early books (erroneously) that "concepts are only found in content—not in skills and processes." But Lois kept nudging me gently to reconsider my position. I finally came to see that she was absolutely correct—processes *do* have concepts, and students need to understand the conceptual relationships within the English language arts standards if they are going to be able to transfer these expectations across situations.

I am especially thrilled that Lois has taken her learning and developed the ideas in this book that truly break out of old curriculum designs. You will love her graphic that shows the Structure of Process to balance the Structure of Knowledge shown in my books. To tell you the truth, I have always been uncomfortable when trying to explain how concept-based curriculum applies to the English language arts area. My Structure of Knowledge graphic never really explained how English language arts fit except through the content of thematic fiction studies. I knew there was a problem. How lucky we all are that Lois Lanning has written this valuable contribution to English language arts! She is my star pupil, my brilliant colleague, and my dear friend. I know you will enjoy her thinking and her teaching.

H. Lynn Erickson

Preface

Several things compelled me to write this book. First, I believe in the value of a high-quality curriculum. Over the course of my years in public education, I have witnessed the negative effects of teachers not having a common, worthwhile document to guide their instruction. Second, I wanted the challenge of explaining the process of designing a quality curriculum that reflects research on human learning in a straightforward manner. Third, I am fascinated by the learning process and relish stretching my mind and testing my understandings. Writing this book definitely accomplished this!

Many of the trials and tribulations of writing a book parallel those that are part of designing a first-rate curriculum. Writing curriculum takes time, patience, perseverance, and thought. While this is bad news for those looking for a quick fix, educators committed to the continuous improvement of teaching and learning identify curriculum as a priority investment.

My goal in writing this book is to share a powerful curriculum design, developed by H. Lynn Erickson, which has made a difference to thousands of educators around the world, and tailor it specifically to the discipline of English language arts.

The underpinnings of my book stay true to Erickson's doctrines but define how they can be accomplished in a process-based discipline. Since most of my educational career has been grounded in literacy, I spent considerable time with dedicated colleagues pondering what a concept-based curriculum design might look like in English language arts. The results are described in this book and have been overwhelmingly positive.

The purpose of this book is not only to share the nuances of designing a concept-based curriculum for English language arts but to provide the reader with an understanding of how curriculum can support teaching to increase the transfer of learning—an important but often elusive instructional intention.

Although this book is written for English language arts curriculum writers, teachers from other areas who have heard me present this work—world language teachers in particular—tell me the design also makes perfect sense for their discipline. There are strong parallels between the two language-based disciplines. Unfortunately, many still perceive second-language acquisition as a process of memorization and practice and do not realize that there are conceptual understandings that will support the retention and transfer of learning. Finally, this book is also intended for administrators and instructional leaders who need to understand the elements of a concept-based curriculum so they can provide the appropriate and necessary support for curriculum implementation.

An overview of the book follows:

Chapter 1 begins with a discussion about the term *curriculum* and why curriculum matters so much. The chapter concludes with an introduction to the rationale for a concept-based curriculum design (Erickson, 2007, 2008).

Chapter 2 delves deeper into the rationale for a concept-based English language arts curriculum. The chapter opens by comparing traditional English language arts curriculum with a concept-based curriculum. Additionally, Chapter 2 points out the distinctions between the Structures of Knowledge and Process. Lynn Erickson's seminal work about concept-based curriculum shows how promoting the active construction of student understanding begins with a curriculum design aligned with what we know about how people learn. Erickson's work focused on the knowledge side of the equation; this book expands Erickson's principles to the consideration of *processes*. Processes are what help mediate the construction of new knowledge and understandings and play an especially important role in language and communication. The illustrations in Chapter 2 help to further explain the interplay between knowledge and process. Chapter 2 is also critical in preparing readers for understanding the subsequent chapters by defining and redefining the key terminology used in concept-based curriculum. Without this foundation, it is easy to get lost in unfamiliar terms. Chapter 2 concludes by highlighting some of the most noteworthy support for concept-based curriculum design.

Many of us like to "just get going" with work that we recognize is going to be cognitively demanding and take time to digest. The sooner we start, the sooner we will reach the end! Chapter 3 warns this is not the case in curriculum development. The work is messy and has many components. Reaping the return on a high-quality curriculum, in terms of changes to instruction and student learning, requires spending time building a foundation that will provide adequate load capacity for the curriculum work ahead.

Chapters 4–8 provide the explicit guidance needed to build expertise in designing a concept-based English language arts curriculum. The thinking behind each step is explained with many examples and words of advice interjected along the way. Steps include how to utilize the Common Core State Standards for English Language Arts in a concept-based curriculum. These chapters are the heart and soul of the book.

Chapter 9 provides examples of model units from different districts and grade levels. These examples help the reader put all the steps together into a connected whole. Additionally, they may serve as springboards to the thinking of curriculum writers using this book.

And finally, Chapter 10 captures some "voices" of the many exceptional professionals I have had the opportunity to work with over the years. May their stories mentor and guide the way for others who are on this rich and rewarding path.

Why this book versus other curriculum design books on the market? I believe this book captures the best of the concept-based model and tailors it to one of the most all-encompassing and essential fields—English language arts. As you read the following chapters, I hope that a new vision for all curriculum can begin to emerge along with a conviction to make that vision a reality for teachers and students.

Acknowledgments

Writing curriculum is a valuable and resource-intense professional development activity for teachers, which is why it is so important for district leaders to "get it right." I lived through many curriculum designs throughout the course of my career. It wasn't until I discovered the work of H. Lynn Erickson that everything I believe important about curriculum design came together for me.

I first met Lynn at a conference in Massachusetts in 1995. Her presentation on concept-based curriculum triggered such an "aha!" moment for me that my mind instantly started racing with possibilities about what teaching and learning could be. I contacted Erickson shortly afterward, she came to my district, and our journey as colleagues and wonderful friends was launched.

Lynn and I have worked closely together for many years now helping educators understand the power of concept-based curriculum and instruction. Her profound insights and compelling ideas continue to bring out the best in my thinking and practice. I am eternally grateful our life paths crossed.

Part I

Preparing for Curriculum Design

1 Curriculum Matters in Teaching and Learning

I t is a bright, crisp day with subtle signs that fall is beginning to overtake the remaining days of summer. I am on my way to class. Teaching this graduate-level curriculum class to aspiring administrators energizes me. A wealth of professional literature explains how fundamental a quality curriculum is to teaching and learning (Hattie, 2009; Marzano, 2003; Schmoker, 2011), so it is a joy to know that future school leaders have an entire course devoted to the topic as part of the administrator certification program. As much as I look forward to these classes, however, I brace myself for the tales I will hear from many of my students about the status of curriculum in their schools. Each year several students share that they work or fulfill internships in districts or schools that have either no curriculum or curriculum so old and neglected that people don't even know where to find it.

The term *curriculum* is often misunderstood. Some educators refer to state standards as "the curriculum." When asking teachers about curriculum, a frequent response is "We must treat the expectations on our state assessments as our curriculum." Or, even if a district curriculum document exists, many educators consider textbooks and programs by various companies and publishers as their curriculum. Confusion about what curriculum really means seems to be on the rise as more and more adjectives are used to describe curriculum: *rigorous, relevant, 21st century, standards-based, concept-based, timeless* and *timely, differentiated, spiral, purposeful* . . . the list goes on. In addition to this mishmash of descriptors there are titles of specialized curricula advocated by various authors and organizations such as Classical Curriculum, Core Knowledge Curriculum, Advanced Placement, and International Baccalaureate. No wonder practitioners get bogged down with the jargon when trying to explain curriculum to a confused parent or community member!

New terms continue to emerge as theories about how people learn are better understood and as more curriculum authors attempt to apply this contemporary knowledge to their writing. According to Glatthorn (1987), it is common for teachers and administrators to focus on a written, taught, and tested curriculum as described in the examples above. When each of these curricula is considered separately, however, there may be a huge alignment problem, or one set of expectations may be sacrificed for another. It has been demonstrated that when districts spend time ensuring their curriculum is aligned with the expectations in standards and assessments, and the district curriculum is utilized across classrooms, there is a positive and significant impact on student achievement (Turner, 2003). In Bean's view, expressed within the ERS (2003) article, when "the" curriculum is coherent as a whole and its parts are unified and connected by that sense of whole, it communicates the larger, compelling purpose. This is the primary reason why a curriculum enables teachers to see the *big picture.* Seeing the whole is essential to understanding what instruction, assessment, and professional development need to be.

Early in my career, a person who had a significant influence on me was Joseph Yukish. He was the professor for several of the courses required for my master's in reading supervision. His classes were challenging, but I still remember them with reverence. I truly enjoyed being pushed because I understood the relevance of the content and the assignments. I learned about the complex process of teaching reading in a manner that gave me a clear sense of the whole and how all the intricate pieces of the process fit together. Dr. Joe's incantation about instruction was "Teach your struggling readers important strategies and skills through the theory of 'whole, part, whole' in the context of authentic literature they can initially access without difficulty and build from there." This truism has guided my thinking ever since.

One of my favorite writers and researchers, David Perkins, also discusses the importance of providing an accessible vision of the big picture (whole) that students can engage in prior to teaching the subsequent, more challenging parts. In his book, *Making Learning Whole* (2009), Perkins argues that education can be transformed through a framework that makes learning whole and coherent before the isolated pieces are dissected. The parts won't make sense without an understanding of the whole.

Much of this book is organized around the thinking and writing of David Perkins. When I first read *Making Learning Whole,* I immediately connected his ideas to my most recent work: teaching others how to design concept-based curriculum (Erickson, 2007, 2008). Perkins's thinking reinforced my advocacy for redesigning English language arts curriculum so that it better advances effective teaching and learning. Although Perkins does not speak to concept-based English language arts curriculum in particular, I see his principles as support for this curriculum design.

CURRICULUM AS THE MASTER PLAN

People who have the responsibility for the care and growth of your financial assets and those who care for your children have a lot in common. You are entrusting others with precious commodities. Both are charting the future for you and your children. How educators deal with this responsibility recently came to light when I squeezed an appointment in on my calendar for a massage. After working 10 minutes on my shoulder, the massage therapist inquired, "Are you a teacher perhaps?" She claimed she can always spot educators because they carry so much stress!

Teachers feel the tremendous weight of their responsibilities. They are held accountable by a variety of constituencies to meeting the needs of all their students while juggling a platter full of other roles and tasks beyond the classroom. When teachers do not have a viable, understandable, relevant curriculum to inform and guide their work, the job becomes even more stressful, difficult, and unclear. Left to their own devices, teachers often turn to textbooks, the Internet, software programs, or other prepackaged lessons and use their best judgment as to whether or not these resources will help their students meet expected standards. Acute differences among teachers' daily lesson plans mean students receive uneven experiences across classrooms, grade levels, and schools within the same system. As students move from one grade or course to the next, the disparities become more problematic. In this scenario, the lack of a quality, coherent curriculum results in lower-than-expected student performance on high-stakes district and state tests even though teachers and students put in significant effort.

Making sure that teachers have a well-designed curriculum as a basis for lesson planning is a basic and essential responsibility of a school district. Without a curriculum as a master plan, teachers teach "stuff" and students learn, but it may not be the right "stuff" or have relevance to what lies ahead. Many write about the critical role curriculum coherence plays in school improvement (Newmann, Smith, Allensworth, & Bryk, 2001). Focused and sustained attention to a quality district curriculum will facilitate teacher collaboration around designing powerful lessons, sharing student work, and working collectively to solve identified problems.

Students will also benefit, as research indicates students of all ages are likely to learn when their experiences connect and build on one another (Bransford, Brown, & Cocking, 1999). In other words, when learning experiences are disconnected, it is far more difficult to realize growth. Coherent lessons help students see the bigger whole, which fuels motivation and engagement.

A "master" curriculum creates a ripple effect. As assessments and instruction become aligned with the curriculum, choices and needs for professional development become clearer. With increased coherence among these elements comes greater clarity about what and how teachers are expected to teach and the support necessary for them to achieve this. Strong program coherence through a district curriculum should not be translated into regimented lessons where every teacher is on the same page on the same day at the same time. There should be room in the curriculum document for differentiation that still follows the curriculum road map. In other words, the curriculum should not be so narrowly defined that it forces all teachers to be one color—beige—but, on the other hand, it should not be so loose or vague about common expectations that a sustained, district-wide focus is lost.

Standards are a first step in promoting coherence. Standards are not the curriculum, however. A long list of standards can quickly become overwhelming to teachers trying to figure out what to teach when. Additionally, standards do not address discipline content or cohesion. A district curriculum organized in a user-friendly manner is a more manageable resource for teachers, and when designed appropriately it provides assurance to teachers that if their instruction follows the curriculum, the standards will be addressed. Curriculum is the "master plan" that makes the picture of the year whole for teachers.

WHAT IS CONCEPT-BASED CURRICULUM?

A conceptually organized, or concept-based, curriculum departs from *traditional* curriculum, which is based primarily on topics, skills, and facts. A concept-based curriculum brings in another dimension because it includes a focus on the *transfer* of the important conceptual ideas of a discipline and facilitates *synergistic thinking* (Erickson, 2008). Erickson defines synergistic thinking as the interactive energy that occurs between the lower- and higher-order processing centers of the brain. To develop the intellect and increase motivation for learning, curriculum and instruction must deliberately create a "synergy" between the lower (factual) and higher (conceptual) levels of student thinking.

"A concept-based curriculum raises the bar for curriculum design, instruction and assessment" (Erickson, 2008, p. 28). When key concepts (ideas) of a discipline become the "drivers" for learning, we lead students to deeper understandings that transfer across different situations. Foundational skills and critical content knowledge (facts) are still important components of a concept-based curriculum; however, the inclusion of concepts leverages student thinking and the retention of learning by bringing relevance to the more complex skills and to the factual examples. Much more about this will be explained in upcoming chapters.

> A **concept-based curriculum** includes a focus on the *transfer* of the important conceptual ideas of a discipline and facilitates *synergistic thinking.*
>
> **Synergistic thinking** is the interactive energy that occurs between the lower- and higher-order processing centers of the brain.

Considering the concepts that need to be included in an English language arts curriculum ultimately moves the dialogue among curriculum writers beyond a list of books and skills to consideration of the essential ideas we want to make sure students understand. For example, students who comprehend the idea of *voice* are more capable as readers in recognizing, appreciating, and evaluating all authors' use of language. Additionally, as writers, there is an understanding about the skills required to create a specific tone or mood in a piece.

Erickson (2008) points out that a conceptual structure for curriculum is important because conceptual understanding requires content knowledge, but the reverse is not necessarily true. By designing curriculum in this manner, teachers are clear about the concepts and understandings that students must master each year. This relates back to the importance of making the "big picture" clear. We cannot assume that all teachers will independently figure out the important ideas of a discipline that will promote deeper understanding and transfer.

A word of caution: Just making teachers aware of a list of important, transferable ideas of a discipline does not directly translate into a quality concept-based curriculum either. If only life could be so simple! Each component of the curriculum is carefully constructed into a coherent "whole" that articulates what students need to understand, know, and be able to do. As you will see, there are multiple layers in the process of concept-based curriculum writing. This is why writing in curriculum teams is essential. Solo curriculum writers are denied the insights and contributions of others, and the end product will reflect this disadvantage.

What a concept-based English language arts curriculum "looks like" and how it is developed are discussed in much greater depth in the chapters ahead. The bottom line is that having a quality curriculum does directly impact the student performance results a district or school will realize. The Common Core State Standards (www.corestandards.org) target the performances students are expected to demonstrate. If we do not design curriculum that provides teachers with a clear, unambiguous picture of *how to teach to understanding,* the Common Core State Standards will become yet another initiative that fails to impact student learning or the state of education in our country.

Perhaps Abigail Marks (personal communication, February 24, 2012), a reflective practitioner from Newtown High School in Newtown, Connecticut, sums it up best:

> In my eight years of teaching, I have worked on curriculum development for several summers and always look forward to the opportunity to review what we do and how we do it. While our curricula have always been aligned with our district standards, informally, my colleagues and I always seem to talk more about the books we are teaching, rather than the skills or concepts. While there's an understanding that we're generally on the same page, I'm surprised every year to discover some teachers of the same grade level teaching skills that I am not, or vice versa.
>
> We were introduced to a concept-based curriculum at the same time that our state adopted the Common Core State Standards. This has been both inspiring and useful in helping us take our existing curricula and merge them with the Common Core. It has made the transition to the Common Core seem less daunting; in fact, I am excited for what concept-based curriculum will do for our department's alignment in the teaching of skills and concepts. We will move forward knowing, rather than assuming, that our students will have a truly vertically aligned learning experience.
>
> I view concept-based curriculum as the foundation upon which each teacher can build experiences and learning activities for his or her specific group of students. I have always valued the ability to make choices as a teacher and have feared uniformity, but I believe that concept-based curriculum will provide a strong sense of unity without stifling creativity and the ability to play off of one's strengths as a teacher.
>
> Abi Marks, High School English Teacher

2

The Components of a Concept-Based English Language Arts Curriculum

Picture this:

You are the new intern assigned to a classroom. You walk in and look around at the walls. They are filled with charts asking questions with students' answers and thoughts listed and revised in different-colored markers. You read with interest some of the responses listed under the question "What is the difference between a character trait and a physical characteristic?" Clearly, the charts are a living part of the learning happening in this classroom.

You also notice the words *character relationships* posted at the front of the room with examples of characters from different books cited. Hmm, not everyone is reading the exact same book in this classroom. Now that is interesting! A variety of student work hangs on the walls with one special section titled "Our Generalizations to Date." Various sentence strips fill this section, and the statements look like conclusions students have drawn about their lessons so far.

The classroom is print rich, filled with books, magazines, and newspapers. Computers are accessible, and students use them independently as needed. Voices buzz as students converse with each other in small groups. They are so focused they don't even notice you. As you wander around a bit, you see the

(Continued)

(Continued)

students in each group are searching for evidence from their particular book to answer this question: "How do authors embed explicit and implicit evidence that helps readers make inferences about characters?" The language students are using makes them sound like experts: "pivotal moment," "voice," "dialogue."

The students are demonstrating their conceptual understanding not only by the words they are using in their conversations, but also by constructing their own responses to the posed question. Not every group is responding in the same manner. One group has designed and is completing a graphic organizer, another is making a list of examples from a book with page numbers cited, and yet another is working out a skit with one student acting as the author being interviewed by the others. The teacher moves from group to group raising questions, reminding groups how much time remains before they need to share their findings with the class, and sometimes pulling a student or two aside for some individual support. You had trouble finding the teacher at first! She continually scans the work all students are doing and frequently references a chart or word on the wall while joining in on a group's lively discussion.

Clearly, the learners in the classroom described above are engaged in work that will serve them well in the future. The lesson specifically guides students' analyses of writers' craft, which in turn strengthens understanding of their own reading and writing. The teacher is structuring her lessons in a purposeful manner that moves content and complex skills to a conceptual level of understanding. In doing so, her students are cognitively stretched and motivated (in part because they are reading text selections they are interested in and can read without frustration). The design of the assignment requires students to *produce* knowledge rather than have it poured into them. The conscious links the teacher makes between the day-to-day activities and the major concepts in the unit of study means students are more likely to successfully transfer their conceptual understandings to new tasks and situations: a critical goal of schooling.

In this chapter, I will define the components of a concept-based English language arts curriculum—a curriculum that can lead to the kind of classroom described above, and the kind of student engagement and learning you witnessed in that snapshot. At times, the terminology may seem overwhelming. Fear not! In subsequent chapters I will break down the process of designing the curriculum into much smaller steps, and will provide you with plentiful examples. This chapter can be used, as needed, as a reference point. I will do my best to make the definitions clear and the ideas sequential. But first, let's see how the curriculum that is driving the instruction described above differs from traditional curriculum and teaching.

TRADITIONAL CURRICULUM, TRADITIONAL TEACHING

As discussed in Chapter 1, some teachers still rely on publishers to tell them what to teach, or rely on a list of books to cover within a prescribed time frame. Kathy Swift (personal communication, February 25, 2012), a long-standing high school English teacher from Newtown, Connecticut, recalls, "In 1984, my first teaching assignment included the courses English II and Creative Writing. Both courses came with a list of books, period. I remember asking which book was for character, which for theme, and so on. 'Whatever I wanted,' was the answer." This approach is especially counterproductive in an era when pressures to meet standards are increasing and as faith in public education is declining. We can turn the tide!

The problem with the traditional structure (and too often the accompanying instruction) of the English language arts curriculum is its inability to keep up with the expanding literacy expectations created by the advent of the microchip. We can no longer ask students to study the processes of reading, writing, speaking, listening, viewing, and presenting as isolated entities. When we drag students through question after question about a single text—one that many in the class may not be interested in—for weeks and weeks, it does not promote understanding. In fact, precious time is consumed, often with minimal return on learning. When we test students on bits of skills or ask them to regurgitate facts, they may receive high marks on the tests but be unable to transfer competency to the next text or learning situation. These conflicting experiences can confuse students and cause them to either give up or work harder to no avail because understanding is lacking.

A curriculum design that guides instruction and assessment by explicitly identifying the conceptual understandings tied to process and content will break this cycle. Raising the bar for English language arts curriculum is a critical first step. Using inquiry and inductive teaching to guide students to conceptual understanding not only creates deeper understanding of text—but also develops personal intellect by stimulating synergistic thinking between the lower levels and higher, conceptual levels of thinking. This engagement of the students' personal intellect also increases their motivation for learning, because each student's personal thinking is valued.

FROM TRADITIONALLY DESIGNED CURRICULUM TO CONCEPT-BASED CURRICULUM DESIGN

Most traditional English language arts curriculum represents a two-dimensional design model. The two dimensions are typically (1) processes, which include the specific strategies and skills students are expected to perform, and (2) content knowledge that students are expected to learn. In order to design a concept-based curriculum, a third dimension, "conceptual understanding," must be represented (Erickson, 2007, 2008; see also Figure 2.1). When students understand, they are able to better retain and transfer their learning. Students may regurgitate information about a particular book and execute routine writing skills, but without deeper conceptual understanding, they will never think, perform, or feel like a more capable and confident reader and writer.

Figure 2.1 Illustration of Two- Versus Three-Dimensional Curriculum

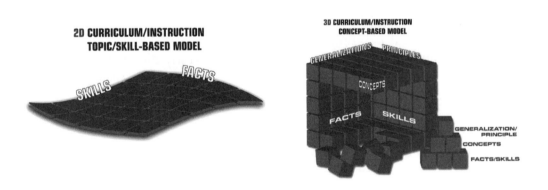

Source: H. Lynn Erickson.

The third dimension, *understanding,* is represented in a concept-based curriculum through concepts and generalizations. We need to understand these critical terms before continuing. First, let's define what a *concept* is. A concept is a mental construct that is

> A **concept** is a mental construct that is timeless, universal, and abstract (to different degrees).

- timeless,
- universal, and
- abstract (to different degrees). (Erickson, 2008, p. 30)

In English language arts, concepts pull thinking beyond the example at hand. To explain in more detail, the concept of "character" is highly abstract for a kindergartener. In response to the teacher's question, a child may correctly *identify* a particular character in a story (skill) but not *understand* "character" as a concept. When teachers continue to provide rich examples of characters across many different types of texts, students begin to see conceptual patterns of the idea of "character." Because concepts are timeless, they were relevant to the discipline years ago, remain relevant today, and will be relevant in the future. Because concepts are universal, examples of the concepts may be found across situations and cultures.

A concept is a noun (never a proper noun or pronoun), may be one to two words, and is represented by different examples that share common attributes. There certainly are many different examples of "characters" across texts, but each example represents fictional individuals with distinctive personalities in a larger imaginary situation, and each individual has a role in moving the story along.

Concepts help organize an English language arts curriculum and are the critical ingredients when writing generalizations for each curriculum unit.

Generalizations are a critical component of a concept-based curriculum. Generalizations are the clear, compelling statements of understanding that will direct instruction and assessments. Some writers refer to generalizations as *enduring understandings*, *essential understandings*, or *big ideas*. Generalizations adhere to the same criteria as concepts. Erickson (2008) defines generalizations as

- broad and abstract;
- universal in application;
- generally timeless (they may need a qualifier if the ideas do not hold up through time in all cases);
- represented by different examples, which support the generalization; and
- two or more concepts, stated in a relationship.

There should be no proper nouns or pronouns in generalizations and no past- or future-tense verbs (so that the statement of understanding is transferable through time and situations).

For example:

The following is *not* a generalization. It is a past-tense statement and refers to a particular character and book, and therefore will not transfer.

> **Generalizations** represent the important, enduring understandings we want students to realize by the end of a unit of study.

The character, Harry, was a hero to many.

To change this into a timeless generalization we might say:

> Readers identify with characters who exhibit personalities or behaviors considered heroic.

Generalizations avoid passive voice. They are strong, clear statements of understanding that represent many examples; however, as mentioned above, sometimes a qualifier (*may, often, can, frequently,* etc.) is necessary because the statement does not hold true across *all* cases.

Erickson (2008) provides us with a simple structure for writing quality generalizations. She suggests starting with the following sentence stem:

> Students will understand that . . .

This stem is later dropped off the generalization. Also, to write a generalization you must *use at least two concepts in a statement of relationship connected with a strong verb.* Avoid weak verbs (*affect, impact, influence, is, have, are*) that result in very broad surface-level statements. You will find more details about generalizations and numerous examples in Chapter 6.

Writing generalizations is often the most challenging aspect of concept-based curriculum development. I have listened to many a teacher struggle while constructing generalizations, but with further discussion (responding to questions of why or how), the ideas are defined more specifically and wordsmithed into powerful statements that are important to students' understanding. Generalizations are scaffolded to high levels of complexity as students advance in their learning. A concept-based curriculum brings out deeper understanding through the curriculum unit generalizations.

Generalizations in English language arts are written to communicate the important understandings about the discipline's processes and content under study. This does not mean that practicing skills is not important! Key skills will be addressed at another point in the curriculum unit and are drawn almost directly from standards, such as the Common Core State Standards for English Language Arts. *If we do not teach to the conceptual understandings (generalizations) behind the more complex, abstract skills and the relationships among concepts in the discipline, we are missing the opportunity to develop students' deeper understanding of English language arts.*

THE RELATIONSHIP BETWEEN KNOWLEDGE AND PROCESS

Think about something you know very well. Is your answer a topic or a process? I have a friend who answered the question like this: "I am a Civil War buff. I know a lot about the subject." I have another good friend who replied, "I know how to garden very well. You should come see my backyard while the weather is still nice!" Let's probe both responses a little further by asking two more questions:

How did you come to understand _____?
How do you know you really understand _____?

Here are the answers from both persons:

I came to understand the Civil War through wide reading. I have probably read over 100 books now related to the Civil War. I have also seen many films and attended every lecture I could on the subject. I know I really understand this topic because I can pose questions that no one else in an audience can, because I readily see analogies between issues in the Civil War and other situations, and because I can converse confidently with someone considered a noted Civil War "expert."

I came to understand gardening primarily by gardening! I also read many different gardening books, talk with a lot of professional gardeners, and visit many diverse gardens locally and in the places I travel. This has been years of learning through practice, understanding gardening techniques, and building my knowledge base. How do I know I understand gardening? The fruits of a gardener's labor are very public! I have had lots of trial and error because there is so much more involved than just memorizing the names of plants and planting things I think are beautiful . . . but . . . well, come look at my garden!

Most of us, and unfortunately too many of our students, forget much of what we have been taught. We tend to remember that which we did *not* understand and how uncomfortable it made us feel. Or, we may remember bits and pieces of our past learning, but the learning may be fraught with misconceptions. How many of us remember all the steps for solving polynomial equations? The majority of us do not remember because while we were in high school solving polynomial equations, we did not see any relevance to the real world. In fact, when was the last time we solved a polynomial equation? Probably in high school! Our memories also fail us because when we were learning about polynomials, we never really understood the concepts behind the formulas or rules. We were "doing" the algorithm without understanding.

Organizing a concept-based curriculum around conceptual questions such as "How does one's identity develop?" supports connected and interesting learning. What's more, when teachers implement the curriculum through authentic literacy experiences that mirror the types of knowledge and processes students will most likely continue to use in their futures, understanding is advanced. Finally, when the curriculum is designed to stimulate thought, reflection, and ownership of learning, students are more motivated to learn, which makes the learning experience far more memorable.

One of the first steps in writing concept-based English language arts curriculum is to develop a map of curriculum unit titles that will resonate with students' interests and concerns and at the same time provide numerous opportunities for teachers to address the expected performance standards and content. For example, a sixth-grade unit title of "How Can We Change the World?" offers endless possibilities for fiction and nonfiction literacy experiences for students to grapple with at a point in their lives when they love a good cause! Within this unit, teachers would teach to "understandings" drawn from text concepts and from English language arts processes. They would also make sure students master the *key skills* and subject-area *knowledge* expected at this grade level. As you can see, there is a relationship among *understanding, knowing,* and *doing.*

Figure 2.2 illustrates this point.

Figure 2.2 Comparison of Structures

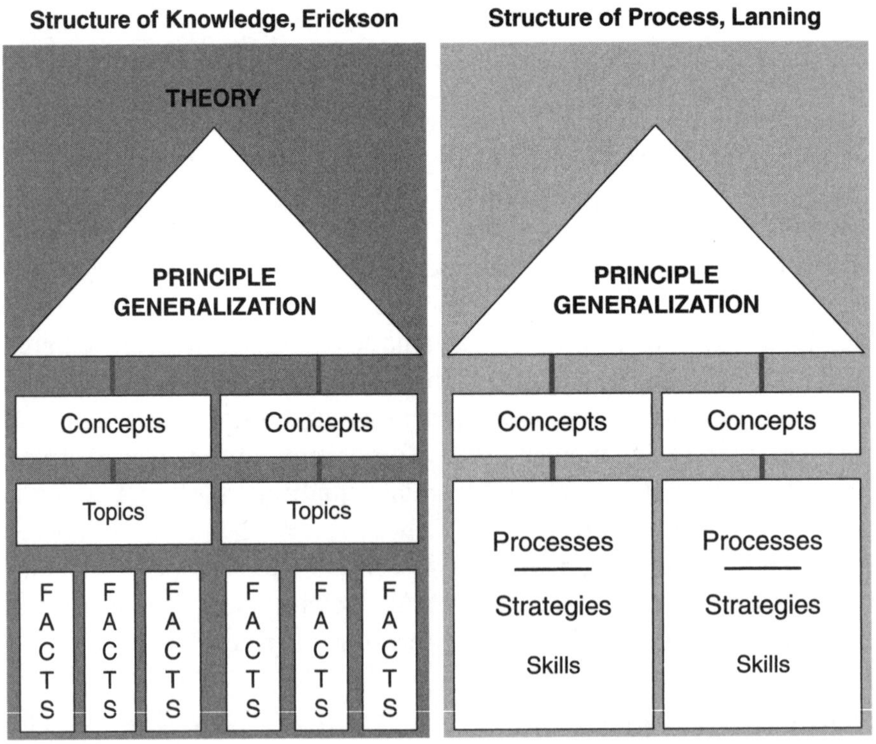

Structure of Knowledge, Erickson

THEORY

PRINCIPLE
GENERALIZATION

Concepts | Concepts

Topics | Topics

F A C T S | F A C T S | F A C T S | F A C T S | F A C T S | F A C T S

Structure of Process, Lanning

PRINCIPLE
GENERALIZATION

Concepts | Concepts

Processes
———
Strategies

Skills

Processes
———
Strategies

Skills

Source: "Structure of Knowledge" from *Stirring the Head, Heart, and Soul: Redefining Curriculum, Instruction, and Concept-Based Learning,* third edition (p. 31), by H. L. Erickson, 2008, Thousand Oaks, CA: Corwin. Reprinted with permission.

UNDERSTANDING THE TWO STRUCTURES

An English language arts curriculum must integrate components of the Structure of Knowledge and the Structure of Process, as both are necessary for a language-based subject area.

Erickson's (2008) *Structure of Knowledge* illustrates the relationship among the components of knowledge. The hierarchy in the Structure of Knowledge represents knowledge of a topic at the lowest cognitive level (factual) up to the highest level of understanding.

My *Structure of Process* illustrates the relationships among the components of *using* knowledge and also represents the hierarchy of processes from the lowest cognitive level to a level of understanding. In other words, this structure builds from the more specific cognitive level (skills) up to a deep understanding of the transferable ideas that are important to a process.

The Structure of Knowledge

The structures depicted in Figure 2.2 represent knowledge and process separately but show the important relationship between them. Erickson (2008) uses the Structure of Knowledge as a rationale for designing concept-based curriculum. The Structure of Knowledge illustrates the relationship of concepts to topics and facts, generalizations, principles, and theories. Before going further, let's take a closer look at Erickson's Structure of Knowledge on the left side of Figure 2.2 and define each of its components:

1. Starting from the bottom of the structure, *facts* are specific pieces of information, locked in time, place, or situation. Traditionally, the majority of content study in American schools has been on the memorization of isolated facts, which is the lowest cognitive level.

2. The next layer up is the *topic* level: A topic reflects the subject of study. Topics identify the content of the unit.

3. Moving up to the next level in the Structure of Knowledge, *concepts* are at a higher level of abstraction than facts. Concepts are drawn from the topic, and they serve as cells for categorizing factual examples. Because concepts are timeless, they provide lessons through the ages that grow in sophistication.

4. The level of *generalization/principle* reflects deep understanding of knowledge. Generalizations are statements that synthesize factual examples and summarize learning. Generalizations are defined formally as two or more concepts stated in a relationship. Although generalizations are timeless, they may not always hold true (unlike a *principle*, which is a law or an axiom—a foundational "truth" of a

discipline). If a generalization is an important idea, but does not always hold true across all situations, then qualifiers such as *often, can,* and *may* are used in the sentence. Concept-based curriculum uses the term *generalization* to represent the important enduring knowledge and principles we want students to come to understand.

5. Finally, we have reached the top of the Structure of Knowledge: A *theory* is a set of statements or principles devised to explain a group of facts or phenomena, especially one that has been repeatedly tested or is widely accepted. A theory is considered a body of principles belonging to a subject area. The atomic theory of matter and the theory of relativity are examples.

Erickson (2008) also makes the point that traditionally in education, the majority of textbooks, curriculum, and instruction have focused on the lower levels of the Structure of Knowledge: topics and facts. To change this, writing a concept-based curriculum begins with a topic and moves *up* the structure before deciding on the factual examples that will be part of students' learning.

First, the important ideas (concepts) of the unit are unpacked from the topic. Next, these concepts are used to write generalizations. Generalizations are the clear, powerful statements of understanding that will guide instruction. The generalizations become the criteria for deciding what facts will best exemplify the understandings. Using the generalizations as learning targets helps curriculum from becoming mired down in an overabundance of factual information. Students need enough examples to realize the generalization but not so many that the learning becomes disconnected and unmemorable. Let's look at an example using the Structure of Knowledge:

1. **Unit Topic:** The American Revolution

2. **Concepts:** Economic oppression, revolution, interdependence/ dependence, freedom, power . . .

3. **Generalization:** Social, political, and/or economic oppression may lead to revolution.

4. **Facts:** Stamp Act of 1765, 13 colonies, Continental Congress . . .

The facts that will be included in this unit are determined after six to eight generalizations are articulated. Once the curriculum is complete and the unit is being taught, students' thinking is moved toward understanding the generalizations through guiding questions and engaging activities that focus on the concepts and utilize facts as examples. It is important to note that teachers *do not* state the curriculum generalizations to students at the beginning of a lesson. Rather, students *discover* the generalizations on their own and state them in their own words (which, when stated, will sound similar to the generalization written in the curriculum). Students will be capable of producing generalizations as a result of instruction that requires them to look for patterns and ideas within the examples presented. This is what makes a concept-based curriculum a thinking curriculum! You may also find some students come up with generalizations that are not written in the unit of study. The list of unit generalizations is not absolute, so when this occurs, it represents conceptually minded students—a goal of concept-based teaching and learning and a cause for celebration.

The Structure of Process

It is time to turn our attention to the second structure in Figure 2.2, depicted on the right. The Structure of Process illustrates the relationship of skills, strategies, processes, concepts, generalizations, and principles.

When we reach the level of concepts in the Structure of Process, we move from "doing" to "knowing and understanding" *why* we do what we do. Concepts are not the act of "doing"—for example, utilizing a process, strategy, or skill—although concepts may be drawn out of each of these operations to support understanding. This will be further explained in Chapter 4. For purposes of explaining the Structure of Process, consider *processes, strategies,* and *skills* as the tools to help students engage with and explore the content under study.

Each component of the Structure of Process is defined below:

1. The bottom of the structure—the lowest level in the Structure of Process—includes *process, strategies,* and *skills.* All three are included in this component, with process being the broadest and most complex, then strategies, and finally skills. Because concepts in English language arts curriculum can be drawn from each, these actions are clustered together in the illustration.

   - *Skills:* Skills are the smaller operations or actions that are embedded in strategies and, when appropriately applied, "allow" the strategies to work. Skills underpin a more complex strategy.
   - *Strategies:* A strategy may be thought of as a systematic plan learners consciously adapt and monitor to improve their learning performance (Harris & Hodges, 1995). Strategies are complex because many skills are situated within a strategy. In order to effectively employ a strategy, one must have control over a variety of the skills that support the strategy, be fluent and flexible in the utilization of these skills, and appropriately integrate other relevant skills and strategies.
   - *Process:* Processes are actions that produce results. A process is continuous and moves through stages during which inputs

(materials, information, people's advice, time, etc.) may transform or change the way a process flows. A process defines what is to be done—for example, the writing process, the reading process, the digestive process, the respiratory process, and so on. These processes are continuous and stop only when an intervention takes place. The quality of the result may be dependent on inputs (as mentioned above). During various stages of a process, inputs may transform the way the process is unfolding, and the result may emerge with different characteristics than originally perceived.

2. Moving up to the next level in the Structure of Process are *concepts,* represented in one to two words (nouns). They characterize the mental constructs or ideas drawn from the content (topics), and from the complex processes, strategies, and skills that are under study. Concepts are used to write statements of understanding (generalization) that we want students to realize by the end of the unit. Consistent with how concepts were previously defined in the Structure of Knowledge, concepts are timeless; they provide lessons through the ages that grow in sophistication. Because they are universal, the representative examples may be derived from any culture.

3. Finally, we reach the triangle:

- *Principle:* A principle is defined as a fundamental rule or truth. In the subject of English language arts, some consider the prescriptive rules of language grammar or usage as principles.
- *Generalization:* Erickson (2008) defines generalizations as statements that are summaries of thought. They answer the relevancy question "What will I understand as a result of my study?" Again, generalizations are defined formally as two or more concepts stated in a relationship. Occasionally, generalizations may need a qualifier added to the statement if the idea is important to the subject of study but may not be verifiable across all situations. To avoid confusion, only the term *generalization* will be used in writing concept-based English language arts curriculum; we will not worry about whether or not a statement of understanding represents a principle or a generalization because that is not the point. The point is to identify the important, transferable understandings we want students to reach by the end of the unit of study.
- *Theory:* Because it is not relevant to the discipline of English language arts, theory is not included in the Structure of Process.

You can see that the terms *concepts* and *generalizations/principles* are included in the Structure of Knowledge and in the Structure of Process. These three terms are defined the same way in both structures and represent the same relationships.

Now, let's look at a quick example of how a generalization would be crafted using the Structure of Process:

1. **Unit Title:** *Information Please!*

2. **Concepts:** Summary, relevant information, text features (bold headings, glossary, diagrams, etc.) . . .

3. **Generalization:** Readers use various nonfiction text features (charts, diagrams, maps, graphs, captions, headings, bold words, etc.) to more efficiently find relevant information and to develop a deeper understanding of a topic.

Additional generalizations in the curriculum unit would include transferable understandings about the content under study, as well as other processes. Again, as this English language arts unit is taught, students' thinking is directed toward understanding the generalizations through guiding questions and engaging activities that focus on the concepts. In Chapter 6, you will find examples of English language arts curriculum integrating components of the Structure of Knowledge and the Structure of Process since both are necessary for this subject area.

SUPPORT FOR THESE STRUCTURES

In *A Taxonomy for Learning, Teaching, and Assessing: A Revision of Bloom's Taxonomy of Educational Objectives* (2001), editors Anderson and Krathwohl explain why the 1956 *Handbook* needed revision. First, with the design and implementation of accountability programs, standards-based curriculums, and authentic assessments, much of the information is still relevant today and worth revisiting. Second, the significant new knowledge and thought that has emerged since the first taxonomy needed to be included in the framework. (Krathwohl, by the way, worked with Bloom and coauthored the original *Handbook*.) The new book explains that Bloom believed each major field should have its own taxonomy of objectives in its own language—more detailed, and closer to the special language and thinking of its experts. It was always expected that the taxonomy would be adapted. The single focus of the original taxonomy was cognitive processes (verbs). In contrast, the updated taxonomy focuses on two dimensions: *process* and *knowledge*. Knowledge is distinct from process, but there is an interrelationship between the two. For example, one may have conceptual knowledge; an understanding of the processes used to access and make sense of this knowledge is represented in the process dimension.

We need to consider both knowledge and processes when designing a concept-based English language arts curriculum. We also need to ensure learning expectations build in sophistication and depth of understanding as they move to the next course or grade level. Anderson and Krathwohl (2001) maintain that students *understand* when they build connections between the "new" knowledge to be gained and their prior knowledge. "More specifically, the incoming knowledge is integrated with existing schemas and cognitive frameworks. Since concepts are the building blocks for these schemas and frameworks, *Conceptual knowledge* provides a basis for understanding" (Anderson & Krathwohl, 2001, p. 70). They also explain that by separating factual knowledge from conceptual knowledge, they are highlighting "the need for educators to teach for *deep understanding of Conceptual knowledge,* not just for remembering isolated and small bits of factual knowledge" (Anderson & Krathwohl, 2001, p. 42).

In *How People Learn* (1999), Bransford, Brown, and Cocking suggest that "organizing information into a *conceptual framework* allows for greater *transfer;* that is, it allows students to apply what they learned to new situations, and it supports learning-related information more quickly" (Bransford et al., 1999, p. 17). The book goes on to stress that "superficial coverage of all topics in a subject area must be replaced with *in-depth coverage of fewer topics* that allows key concepts in that discipline to be understood" (Bransford et al., 1999, p. 20). "The fact that experts' knowledge is organized around *important ideas or concepts* suggests that curricula should also be organized in ways that lead to *conceptual understanding*" (Bransford et al., 1999, p. 42).

PROVIDING A ROAD MAP FOR INSTRUCTION

This chapter discussed some of the underpinnings of a concept-based curriculum design. In order to understand the classroom instruction described at the beginning of this chapter, one must have confidence in the research and curriculum design that supports and directs the teaching. A wealth of professional literature exists on instructional delivery that supports transfer. The missing piece, until the past couple of decades, has been how to design a curriculum that will provide the right road map for the instruction. The components of a concept-based English language arts curriculum are specifically written so teachers are clear about what students need to understand, know, and be able to do to meet and exceed grade- or course-specific standards.

Now that you have an understanding of the whole picture—the type of curriculum we are striving for—the next chapter will specifically describe the preliminary work of the curriculum writing process.

3 Getting Started

Doing the Preliminary Work

Curriculum work is a messy process. Many questions are raised when districts or schools decide to develop a new curriculum. The first question is typically "Where do we begin?" Reviewing the influences that support successful change or contribute to its demise is a good place to start.

Writing a new curriculum means changing, and change is not easy for most people. Individuals have very different reactions when they hear about a proposal for change. Anxiety, fear, anticipation, and apprehension may arise when teachers hear the English language arts curriculum will be changing, especially if it is an unfamiliar design. The new curriculum directly affects teachers' work, so an emotional response is legitimate. The way curriculum leaders connect and communicate with all stakeholders throughout the process will determine how successful the change will be.

LEADING CURRICULUM CHANGE

Much is written about the change process. Do a Google search of the words *change process*, and over 2 million hits will pop up! We know a lot about change but continue to see the best of intentions fail. Did you know that over 90% of people who have bypass surgery return to their old ways of eating and a sedentary lifestyle after one year? I learned this amazing fact while attending a training session on *leading bold change*. The training was based on a book by John Kotter and Holger Rathgeber (2005), *Our Iceberg Is Melting: Changing and Succeeding Under Any Conditions*. This book is a short, easy-to-read, fun fable that outlines a well-researched eight-step change method representing the best thinking about how to succeed in an era of change. If you are unfamiliar with theories of change, it may be worthwhile to spend some time building your background knowledge in these theories before venturing to lead a major curriculum change initiative. As mentioned above, there is an abundance of information available. Although this book is not about the change process, the suggestions within are aligned with what change research tells us.

Plateaus or declines in student test results, changes in student demographics, new leadership, increasing demands for accountability, new learning in the field of education, and/or revised state or district standards are just a few of the factors that can create an urgent need for curricular change. When the urgency for change is genuine, designing a curriculum that will address the problems requires a serious and multiyear commitment from a curriculum leadership team.

ASSEMBLING THE CURRICULUM LEADERSHIP TEAM

Teamwork is at the core of complex work that impacts an organization. It takes more than one person or published program to truly transform teaching and learning. Selecting the right curriculum leadership team is a critical step and should not be taken lightly. These are the people who will lead the change; they will also help with ongoing communications, decision making, and feedback.

The following are features of a successful team and its members:

- The team represents the various constituencies and diversity of the system (all school levels, classroom teachers and specialists, administrators, etc.).
- The team has credibility and sufficient influence with staff.
- The team includes members with different perspectives, but all participants are able, and must agree, to check any personal agendas at the door. They put the interests of the district and its students first.
- Team members are emotionally committed to the successful implementation of the curriculum. Team members hold the good of the organization at heart and respect and value other team members.
- Team members represent a range of experiences and a high degree of expertise. They have knowledge of the standards and expectations of other curriculum areas. They ultimately strengthen the curriculum so it is viable and relevant to all users.
- Team members understand that everyone in the group has an equal voice.
- Team members have excellent analytical capabilities and a willingness to help build a network of curriculum contributors among teachers.

Trust is critical to an effective team. Differences of opinion are openly shared and discussed at team meetings, but once consensus is reached on a decision, everyone needs to stand behind the team. Nothing will erode a team faster than a member betraying team confidentiality or rejecting agreements made at a meeting.

Being a member of the English language arts leadership team provides rich opportunities for personal growth in leadership and collaboration. A leadership team with members from all levels of the organization helps ensure coherence within and across grade levels and schools so that students are well prepared for their future.

The English language arts leadership team will make important, preliminary decisions that set the stage before the actual writing process is launched. Their decisions will enable the work to begin in earnest later, when more teachers participate in actual curriculum development.

The leadership team's first four tasks are these:

1. Articulating a vision

2. Determining the curriculum template

3. Developing strong unit titles

4. Mapping out units of study for the new curriculum

In the following pages, I will detail the steps involved in completing each task.

Articulating a Vision

The first activity for the leadership team is to begin clarifying the future curriculum through the development of a district English language arts vision or philosophy statement. This is an exercise that may take a meeting or two with revisions continuing for some time.

1. **Ask team members to write down the fundamental beliefs they have about literacy learning in their district.** Each belief statement should represent one idea and be written on a separate sticky note or note card. "I believe" statements begin to flush out the core values of the culture—what people hold sacred. The statements allow for wonderful group conversation and instant personal connection to the work that lies ahead.

2. **Display the note cards on a large table.**

3. **Have team members rearrange the cards into categories and reach consensus on the categories.**

4. **Recruit a "first drafter" from the group.** This person takes a stab at incorporating the ideas into the first draft of a vision statement. The draft is brought to the next team meeting where it is read and discussed.

5. **Select a "next drafter" to incorporate the group's suggestions and edits into a second-draft vision statement.** This process continues for several rounds.

6. **Team members split up and share the draft vision with English language arts staff at each school and with each department.** The leadership team members are responsible for helping others understand how the vision statement evolved and how it reflects the desired future state of the English language arts curriculum. Team members gather staff reactions.

7. **Team members bring the feedback they receive to the full leadership team.** The revision process continues until everyone agrees, "This is it!" Often it is one or two words that are tweaked toward the end of the process that results in just the right vision statement.

This document becomes a guide to future curriculum decision making, and a valuable tool for communicating with parents and staff. Figure 3.1 is an example of one district's philosophy statement that evolved using the process described above.

Figure 3.1 Sample District English Language Arts Philosophy Statement

 POMPERAUG REGIONAL SCHOOL DISTRICT 15
Serving the Communities of Middlebury and Southbury, Connecticut

Region 15's K–12 English/Language Arts Curriculum Philosophy Statement

The goal of Region 15's English/Language Arts Curriculum is to foster self-directed learning, effective communication and active participation in a diverse literacy community. To achieve this goal, we begin by recognizing that students have a range of experiences which influence their learning, and that they live in a world demanding high levels of literacy in a variety of formats. Students must be able to think critically, process efficiently, and integrate appropriately the vast amount of information that they are exposed to daily.

The K–12 curriculum supports a process-oriented approach toward student learning of the concepts and skills needed to comprehend and communicate through reading, writing, speaking, presenting, listening, and viewing. The curriculum is best taught through instruction that provides a variety of authentic experiences and student choice. As the dimensions of literacy expand, students have more opportunities to discover themselves as readers and writers.

Students need many opportunities to select, interact with, reflect on, and critique a diverse range of high quality texts that support and challenge their individual development. Similarly, students need to create and reflect on written text and oral presentations across a variety of genre[s], audiences and purposes. These experiences are designed to achieve our curriculum goal and ignite a life-long passion for literacy.

May 1, 2009
Assistant Superintendent's Office

Source: © Pomperaug Regional School District 15.

Determining the Curriculum Template

Districts sometimes mandate that the curriculum template be in the same format across all subject areas and grade levels. The highest priority is that all concept-based curricula include the nonnegotiable components (to be explained in the specific curriculum writing steps in the next chapter) that make a significant difference in teaching and learning. The various unit components can be arranged in a variety of formats. It makes sense to have a consistent format within a particular discipline; however, some disciplines may lend themselves to a slightly different template. Typically, this is a decision the leadership team makes after completing the following steps:

1. Collect and review different unit template models from teachers, other districts, and Internet sites. A suggested template is included in this book in Chapter 9.

2. Discuss which template format best lends itself to the unique expectations of the subject area. Elements of some models may be blended with other ideas that emerge from the discussion.

3. Share the selected template with classroom teachers. Help teachers understand how classroom lessons will be developed from the template, and solicit suggestions. The curriculum template needs to make sense to teachers because they are the implementers of the curriculum. Allowing teachers' voice in the template provides ownership of the curriculum early on in the change process and, consequently, greater commitment to use the new curriculum when it is completed.

4. Know that once the template is finalized, professional development at the point of implementation will be important.

Developing Strong Unit Titles

Most English language arts curricula are now organized by *units of study*. In the past, English language arts curriculum and standards frequently consisted of a disorganized list of discrete skills that teachers struggled to incorporate into their instruction. The Common Core State Standards, and most state English language arts standards, are now written with a specific and strong progression of literacy expectations that emphasize the interpretation of multiple texts or collections of texts. Organizing English language arts curriculum as units lends itself to the Common Core State Standards' increased focus on the synthesis and comparative evaluation and analysis of multiple texts.

Curriculum units must identify the specific subject matter to be learned in addition to the performance expectations. Because deep, transferable understanding is the goal of concept-based curriculum, the subject matter implied in the title of each unit is the vehicle for thought, reflection, analysis, understanding, and skill development. The Common Core State Standards for English Language Arts reference a few specific unit topics (e.g., mythology, foundational U.S. documents, Shakespeare) and go on to state, "The Standards must therefore be complemented by a well-developed, content-rich curriculum consistent with the expectations laid out in this document" (Common Core State Standards Initiative, 2010, p. 6).

In order to meet the standards, students need to have experiences with many different types of texts. As students move on to middle school and high school, the standards increase the percentage of nonfiction texts students must experience. Additionally, many of the performance expectations in the Common Core State Standards call for close reading of challenging texts and considerable writing. The implication of all this is that the English language arts curriculum unit titles need to be substantial enough to address topics that can be unpacked and critically analyzed. Before you begin I strongly suggest the following:

1. **Spend time becoming familiar with how your state standards or the Common Core State Standards for English Language Arts are constructed,** and with the progression of expectations through the grade levels. This is a must for the leadership team. In the past, few practitioners were aware of standards beyond their particular grade level, but understanding how the standards build on one another will enable teachers to see the relevance of the expectations at their particular level.

2. **Conduct an inventory of the curriculum teachers are currently teaching.** This is a necessary strategy for identifying gaps and redundancies in content and expectations when compared to the Common Core State Standards. An initial curriculum inventory also helps to identify the literacy resources that are presently available. This exercise can be accomplished fairly efficiently with a knowledgeable leadership team. The current curriculum may provide some unit titles that can be used in the new curriculum, depending on how old the current English language arts curriculum is. Additionally, when considering the new curriculum, teachers who have worked with students at a specific grade level for any length of time are quick to brainstorm English language arts unit titles that reflect content students will find interesting. Skimming across content that is not compelling to students does little to engage them intellectually or emotionally. Teaching fewer units over the course of the year for longer

periods of time provides more return on investment, so teachers can truly teach for depth of understanding.

Strong unit titles meet the following criteria:

- Represent a range of real-life dilemmas, thought-provoking ideas, and genres that will capture kids' attention and curiosities, and help engage students who are bored and disconnected.
- Build on and challenge students' existing knowledge rather than represent content they need to "get through."
- Provoke inquiry and new perspectives.

A third-grade unit titled "Making Friends and Keeping Friends" clearly fits these criteria. Any teacher who has worked with third graders knows this is a critical grade for peer relationships—who is going to play with whom at recess? What sixth grader could resist getting pulled into a unit titled "How Can We Change the World?" Sixth graders love a cause they can relate to and get behind. The unit "Navigating Global Voices" at the high school level invites all kinds of possibilities. These unit titles allow for a rich array of content across a variety of genres.

Traditional English language arts teachers may initially make the mistake of generating a unit title that represents an isolated process. For example, a unit titled "Grammar" does not represent engaging subject matter. It is essential that students learn about grammar; however, specific grammar knowledge and skills will be articulated in a later section of each of the units.

Generating the right content for units of study will help students know how to confront some of the personal and social challenges they are faced with in our increasingly complex and diverse world. Using inviting subject matter as a vehicle for literacy learning helps students find meaningful connections to content and brings relevance to the knowledge, key skills, and understandings they will be learning. Since the Common Core State Standards ask that students learn how to read closely and learn how to argue, discuss, and compare evidence from multiple texts, we need units of study that are worth digging into and that lend themselves to lively critique. A final reason, not to be overlooked, is teachers will find these units much more interesting and fun to teach! This makes change all the more palatable.

Mapping Out Units of Study for the New Curriculum

1. The leadership team assumes responsibility for the first draft of the district's English language arts curriculum unit map. If your state

has adopted the Common Core State Standards, it would be wise for everyone to first read the standards for English language arts, particularly what they have to say about building knowledge through units of study:

> Building knowledge systematically in English language arts is like giving children various pieces of a puzzle in each grade that, over time, will form one big picture. At a curricular or instructional level, texts—within and across grade levels—need to be selected around topics or themes that systematically develop the knowledge base of students. Within a grade level, there should be an adequate number of titles on a single topic that would allow children to study that topic for a sustained period. The knowledge children have learned about particular topics in early grade levels should then be expanded and developed in subsequent grade levels to ensure an increasingly deeper understanding of these topics. Children in the upper elementary grades will generally be expected to read these texts independently and reflect on them in writing. However, children in the early grades (particularly K–2) should participate in rich, structured conversations with an adult in response to the written texts that are read aloud, orally comparing and contrasting as well as analyzing and synthesizing, in the manner called for by the *Standards*.
>
> Preparation for reading complex informational texts begins at the very earliest elementary school grades by developing curriculum units that focus on building students' conceptual understanding about the reading process. (Common Core State Standards Initiative, 2010, p. 33)

2. The leadership team reviews the suggested unit titles and begins to complete a yearlong map, by grade level, as shown in Table 3.1.

The initial unit map provides an overview of the proposed unit titles for the year by grade level (remember Chapter 1's discussion of keeping the whole in mind?). A K–12 unit map is an important communication tool for change. It allows a holistic view of what lies ahead and how all the units fit together. This overview helps teachers plan their instruction and serves as an effective tool for communicating and evaluating curriculum. Heidi Hayes Jacobs has authored several books that discuss curriculum mapping in depth. At different points in the curriculum development process, the leadership team will need to decide how extensive the mapping

Table 3.1 Sample English Language Arts Curriculum Map

POMPERAUG REGIONAL SCHOOL DISTRICT 15
Serving the Communities of Middlebury and Southbury, Connecticut

Region 15's K–12 Language Arts Units of Study

Grade Level	Unit 1 (Title)	Unit 2 (Title)	Unit 3 (Title)	
K	Part 1: Becoming a Reader and Writer	Part 2: Becoming a Reader and Writer		
1	I'm a Reader and a Writer	What Makes a Story?	Author's Study	
2	Getting to Know Characters	Comparing What We Read and How We Read It	Ingredients of a Mystery	
3	Unit 1: Making Friends, Keeping Friends	Unit 2: Navigating Narrative Nonfiction and Expository Nonfiction	Unit 3: What Is Folklore?	Unit 4: Exploring Memoirs
4	Characterization: Understanding Characters Through Fiction and Characterization: Understanding People Through Biography	Unit 2: Celebrating Poetry!	Unit 3: Informational Reading (nonfiction)	Unit 4: Fantasy
5	Characters and People in Conflict	Nonfiction:w Ready, Set, Research!	Historical Fiction	

(Continued)

(Continued)

POMPERAUG REGIONAL SCHOOL DISTRICT 15
Serving the Communities of Middlebury and Southbury, Connecticut

Region 15's K–12 Language Arts Units of Study

Grade Level	Unit 1 (Title)	Unit 2 (Title)	Unit 3 (Title)	Unit 4 (Title)
6	Relationships Shape Us	Feature Articles: Finding the Gist! (nonfiction)	Short Stories	How Can We Change the World?
7	Historical Fiction: Time Travel Through Literature	Media as a Persuasive Force	Human Nature: Finding Universal Human Traits in Various Forms of Fiction (Realistic Fiction, Science Fiction, Fantasy)	Poetry
	(Power of Voice - ongoing throughout the school year) →			
8	1. The Power of Voice	2. Mystery	3. Perspectives of Coming of Age	4. Humanity Versus Inhumanity

POMPERAUG REGIONAL SCHOOL DISTRICT 15
Serving the Communities of Middlebury and Southbury, Connecticut

Region 15's K–12 Language Arts Units of Study

Course	Unit 1	Unit 2	Unit 3	Unit 4
English I— I read and write to understand myself . . . my life as a literate person.	Identity: Reading With Freedom	Identity: Writing Freely	Identity: Choices Within text	Identity: Listening and Speaking
English II— I read and write to understand other people, places, and times.	Humanity: Hearing the voices of others and one's self	Humanity: Reconciling the voices of others with one's own	Humanity: Discerning the voices of others with one's own	Humanity: Communicating our voices in a world of others
English III— I read and write to understand the role of language in a democracy: American voices.	Voices From the American Edge	Conflicting American Voices	Opportunity and the American Voice	Reliability of American Voices
English IV— I read, write, and create to participate in and affect our global society.	Global Issues and Media Literacy	Navigating Global Voices	Second Semester Senior Elective Block	

Source: © Pomperaug Regional School District 15.

process needs to be to continually support, communicate, and monitor curriculum and instruction.

3. Soliciting staffs' reaction to the proposed titles in the unit map provides a venue for valuable teacher feedback and suggestions before the map is finalized. This consistent back-and-forth communication (from district leadership team, to school, back to district leadership team) is instrumental to the change process. Although you will never get 100% agreement, teachers will often offer insights the team may not have considered. For example, it is not unusual to learn that although a suggested unit sounds terrific, finding resources for the unit would be very challenging.

4. There are several other considerations for the English Language Arts leadership team when drafting a unit map. As the leadership team grapples with each of these questions, they shape a collective commitment to the units of study:

- How many units should there be at each grade level? (Go for fewer units with deeper learning vs. too many units resulting in curriculum overload and superficial exposure.)
- What drives the unit titles? A genre? A book? An author(s)? A conceptual idea or theme? A process? (The pros and cons of each model need to be thoroughly discussed.)
- Will the units be interdisciplinary (integrated across multiple subjects) or intradisciplinary (specific to the subject)?
- What resources are currently available for the units? What resources will be needed?
- How will the progression of units, from kindergarten through Grade 12, build in complexity?

As team members discuss the second question above, they will begin to see there are advantages and disadvantages to each type of unit. For example, deeply studying a genre, such as historical fiction, gives students an understanding of the nuances and features of a specific category of books. This understanding and knowledge increases students' reading comprehension in the genre. When students understand how a genre "works," they can also incorporate the patterns in structures, vocabulary, and audience expectations into their own writing. The specific genre units included at some of the grade levels also provide opportunities for digging into interesting similarities and differences among multiple texts and authors within a genre. Finally, an awareness of the elements of a genre increases students' appreciation for all that the genre entails.

On the other hand, providing ample time for students to study and explore many different texts within a genre unit takes time. If all units are genre studies, there needs to be a considerable number of units included at a grade level each year; otherwise students may not be introduced to a new genre (or revisit a familiar genre) for several years down the road. That brings us back to the issue of breadth versus depth.

When units are organized around a *conceptual idea, question, or process,* a variety of genres may be blended within the unit so that students become aware of the distinctions among types of genres. However, if *all* the units of study are represented in this more general manner, students are robbed of the occasional, intimate study of a specific genre. As you can see in Table 3.1, the district that developed this unit map solved the dilemma by incorporating units of study that include genre, authors, conceptual ideas, and process in order to capitalize on the advantages of each. The main thing to remember is this: A unit will be highly motivating for students if it is engaging and worthy of their attention.

5. The leadership team assembles a curriculum *writing* team.

Sometimes a posting of curriculum writing work is the best way to recruit teachers (see Figure 3.2). Which teachers to include is dependent on funding and the scope of the curriculum work to be done. Ideally, the curriculum is written by teams of teachers from kindergarten through Grade 12. Working as a system provides a significant advantage in promoting coherence and commitment. These are important decisions over which the leadership team may not have control.

If the method of recruiting curriculum writers is a posting, the posting should include:

- The number of days the teachers will work
- The compensation rate
- The importance of committing to *all* of the scheduled days
- Information about how the leadership team will select the curriculum writers
- A brief statement from the applicants that describes their past curriculum writing experiences and why they are interested in working on the new curriculum

Figure 3.2	Posting for K–12 Language Arts Curriculum Writing

TO: K–12 Teachers

RE: Summer 2012 Curriculum Writing–Language Arts

DATE: Tuesday, May 29, 2012

POSTING DATE: Tuesday, May 29, 2012

DEADLINE: Friday, June 15, 2012

K–12 Language Arts Curriculum Writing
Funding will only allow four people total per grade level.
Priority will be given to balancing representation across schools.

High School–Media Center
8:30 a.m. to 2:00 p.m. (each day)
Monday, June 25, 2012, and Tuesday, June 26, 2012
(half-hour break–please bring your own lunch)

Hourly Rate: (contracted rate) × 5 hours per day

To Apply: Send a brief letter of interest including grade level, school location, and experiences that support participation in curriculum writing to asstsuper@centraloffice.org.

Questions may be directed to your building language arts instructional leader or to the assistant superintendent's office at (200) 750–8000, ext. 114.

Notice of Participation: Before the close of the school year, an e-mail will be sent out to teachers selected to participate. District-wide curriculum writing teams will be created that represent all grade levels and schools.

cc: Language Arts Instructional Leaders

More about the curriculum writing team follows in the introduction to Part II.

Seeing the big picture via the curriculum map truly gets everyone excited early on and gets people thinking about possibilities, but remember to allow flexibility and fluidity in the map throughout the process of writing the units of study!

REVIEW OF CONCEPT-BASED CURRICULUM

Now, the leadership and curriculum writing teams are ready to review concept-based curriculum vocabulary and move forward using the steps laid out in Chapters 4–8, which are all about designing the curriculum. The heavy cognitive lifting that we expect our students to do in classrooms will now be expected from all members of the curriculum team!

As you begin this design work, thinking about concepts in English language arts and writing generalizations may feel foreign. The professional development of the leadership and curriculum writing teams is just as important as the professional development of all the curriculum users. Members of the leadership team need to be well equipped to handle some of the intense dialogues that are part of the messy curriculum writing process. Lynn Erickson's (2007, 2008) books about concept-based curriculum coupled with this book will be resources the team will want to return to as the work moves forward.

SUMMARY

Curriculum writing is a multifaceted process and assumes considerable change. People are being asked to behave in new ways and to give up some of their past practices. Curriculum changes directly impact teachers' work; therefore, emotions are aroused quickly. Leaders need to be sensitive and aware as they move the English language arts curriculum vision forward. Some teachers may be more concerned than others about the new curriculum, but hopefully many will be excited about the possibilities.

Before more teachers are invited to the curriculum writing table, the leadership team has some critical work to attend to that will help support successful change. The preliminary work of the leadership team described in this chapter will help ensure the curriculum initiative gets off to a positive start, clearly articulating the vision and establishing the basic curriculum structures. The leadership team empowers others by inviting more teachers to participate in the development of English language arts curriculum units that will make a profound difference in students' literacy learning.

Teaching for understanding, David Perkins (2009) reminds us, encourages teachers to focus their instruction around "generative topics," or topics that are essential to the discipline, resonate with students' interests and concerns, and provide opportunities for great insight and new applications. "Our most important choice is what we try to teach" (Perkins, 2009, p. 61). Each unit in the English language arts curriculum needs to support literacy learning that is memorable and exciting.

A concept-based curriculum is designed with these ideas in mind and is fundamental to teaching for transferable understanding. The introduction to Part II provides an overview of the whole—all of the steps necessary to design a concept-based English language arts curriculum. Chapters 4–8 guide you through each step in detail. Your foundation is in place, so get ready to begin writing!

Part II

An Introduction to the Design Process

In *Stirring the Head, Heart, and Soul*, Lynn Erickson (2008) outlines how to design a concept-based instructional unit for interdisciplinary or intradisciplinary curricula. This book uses Erickson's work as a foundation and customizes the design process specifically for English language arts.

All the steps for designing a concept-based curriculum are listed on page 40. In Part II of this book, I will guide you through one or more steps in each chapter.

As is the case with most complex processes, unit planning is not always a straightforward, linear task. The steps in this book are laid out in a natural order because each step builds toward the next. You will, however, move back and forth among the steps as the unit writing begins to take shape.

ASSEMBLING THE CURRICULUM WRITING TEAM

Below are suggestions, which extend the ideas presented at the end of Chapter 3, for assembling a curriculum writing team.

- After applications are received and reviewed for the posted curriculum writing work (if a posting was done), the leadership team selects members for the curriculum writing team.
- Each grade-level team should include representatives from different schools, if possible, so that everyone sees this work as a system-wide commitment and learns the process together. It is rewarding to see

Steps for Designing Concept-Based English Language Arts Units

Step 1: Create the unit title.

Step 2: Identify the conceptual lens that will focus the unit and support synergistic thinking.

Step 3: Web out the unit's subtopics and concepts around the four strands, *understanding text, responding to text, critiquing text,* and *producing text.* After brainstorming the web, underline the concepts so they will be easily accessed in the next step.

Step 4: Write the generalizations that you expect students to derive from the unit of study. Make sure the generalizations follow the criteria of a quality generalization.

Step 5: Brainstorm the guiding questions that will be used to facilitate the students' thinking toward the generalizations. Guiding questions should be coded as to type (factual, conceptual, provocative).

Step 6: Identify the critical content that students must know by the end of the unit.

Step 7: Identify the key skills that students must exhibit by the end of the unit.

Step 8: Write the common, culminating assessment that will reveal students' understanding of an important generalization(s), and their knowledge of critical content and key skills. Develop a scoring guide, or rubric, with specific criteria teachers should look for when evaluating students' tasks.

Step 9: Roll out *suggested* learning experiences that will ensure students are prepared for the expectations of the culminating assessment and reflect teaching for understanding. Suggestions are examples of learning experiences that address what students should understand, know, and be able to do by the end of the unit, and they are meaningful and authentic. Also, included in this section may be ideas for pacing, during-unit assessments, differentiation, and unit resources.

Step 10: Write the unit overview (in student language) as an introduction to the unit that will grab students' interest and attention.

all grade levels of classroom teachers interacting with and helping one another—often this is the first opportunity a high school teacher may have to work with an elementary teacher!

- An attempt should be made to balance veteran and new teacher participation in the curriculum writing process.
- Invite literacy specialists and special education, library media, and technology teachers to the curriculum writing table. When specialists are well versed in the new curriculum expectations, instructional coherence is strengthened. Specialists also bring unique perspectives to Step 9 of the writing process, designing learning experiences. For example, specialists bring the expertise of how to embed the appropriate use of technology and how to best differentiate learning experiences.
- Grade-level groups should ideally be made up of three to six teachers.
- The total group should have a maximum of 35 to 40 members as too many writers can become unwieldy for the leadership team.

THE ROLE OF THE LEADERSHIP TEAM

Once this large group is assembled, they will need the assistance of members from the leadership team to begin their unit writing. The leadership team often launches the work with a review of the English language arts vision statement, the format of the curriculum template, and the K–12 curriculum map explaining that these documents may need to be "tweaked" as the work unfolds, but they provide the essential structure for getting the work off the ground.

When the writing process begins, the curriculum leadership team members need to intersperse themselves across the grade-level groups of three to six teachers. This helps give recognition to the curriculum leaders and enables them to reinforce the process and emphasize the rationale for the preliminary decisions with other staff members across the district.

Writing curriculum is a valuable and meaningful professional development activity for teachers. Because this work is as much about developing teachers' thinking and understanding as it is about creating a new curriculum, the curriculum writing process takes time. It is not a simple "fill in the blank" type of curriculum. Rather it requires significant thought, discussion, and new learning.

UNIT PLANNING PAGES

The template on pages 42–48 provides a set of unit planning pages as a suggested format and will serve as a guide as you work through the steps of the writing process. A printable version of this form is located at www.corwin .com/conceptbasedcurriculumK-12.

Visit the companion website for a blank "Concept-Based Curriculum Unit Template."

Concept-Based Curriculum Unit Template

K–12 English Language Arts Curriculum

Grade: _____

Unit: _____

Title: _____

Date: _____

Grade Level: _____

Unit Title:

Conceptual Lens:

Understanding Text:

Responding to Text:

Unit Title:

Producing Text:

Critiquing Text:

Grade Level: _____

Unit Title:

Conceptual Lens:

Unit Overview (an engaging summary to introduce students to the unit work):

Technology Integration (What skills do teachers or students need to use this?
How much knowledge or familiarity with the use of the Internet and tools are necessary?):

Standards addressed in this unit:

Grade Level: _____

Unit Title: _____

Generalizations	Guiding Questions (F = factual; C = conceptual; P = provocative)

Source: Adapted from Erickson, 2008.

Critical Content and Key Skills

Critical Content *What Students Will Know*	Key Skills *What Students Will Be Able to Do*
Understanding Text:	**Understanding Text:**
Responding to Text:	**Responding to Text:**
Critiquing Text:	**Critiquing Text:**
Producing Text:	**Producing Text:**

Grade Level: _____

Suggested Timeline	Suggested Learning Experiences (The teacher may . . .)	Assessments (Suggested and Required**)	Differentiation (For Support and Extension)	Resources

Key Resources:

E: Easy   C: Challenging
T: Typical for this time of year   MT: Mentor text

Culminating Unit Assessment

WHAT?

WHY?

HOW?

4 Designing the Curriculum: Steps 1 and 2

At the end of the introduction to Part II, I provided you with a unit planning template that will serve as a guide as you work through the steps of the writing process. In this chapter we will tackle Steps 1 and 2, which you can fill in on the top part of the template shown on page 43.

STEP 1: CREATING A UNIT TITLE

As discussed in Chapter 3, an English language arts unit title might be a conceptual idea that is going to be explored (e.g., "Humanity Versus Inhumanity"), it might be a specific genre (e.g., "Whodunit? Exploring Mysteries!"), or it might be an author study (e.g., "Shakespeare Comes Alive"). The curriculum unit map lists the titles that were discussed and suggested by the district leadership team (with teacher input) during the preliminary work for each grade level across the year (see "Mapping Out Units of Study for the New Curriculum" in Chapter 3). After completing the cover page of the template, insert the unit title into the center of the planning web. The title represents the content that will be studied in the unit.

STEP 2: IDENTIFYING A CONCEPTUAL LENS

The second step is to identify a *conceptual lens* that will integrate and focus the unit. What is a conceptual lens?

- A conceptual lens is a macro concept that serves to integrate students' thinking at a conceptual level so they can more readily see patterns and connections among ideas and across examples.
- A lens is the perspective through which the facts and concepts of a particular unit are viewed and assimilated. The unit's conceptual lens becomes a tool to think with, or to assist thinking, while exploring the content under study.
- A lens provides a *focus* for thinking about the unit.

We can only pay attention to so much. Sternberg (1996) defines attention as "the phenomenon by which we actively process a limited amount of information from the enormous amount of information available through our senses, our stored memories, and other cognitive processes" (p. 69). Knowing this, curriculum and instruction design must try to *optimize* and *direct* students' attention to what is important. This is where the conceptual lens of the unit helps; it directs attention to a selected aspect of the content and to specific complex processes in the unit.

> A **conceptual lens** is a macro concept that serves to integrate students' thinking at a conceptual level so they can more readily see patterns and connections among ideas and across examples.

Erickson (2008) explains that curriculum and instruction must create a *synergy* between the lower levels and conceptual levels of thinking to engage the intellect. The *conceptual lens* supports synergistic thinking by providing a conceptual focus that will guide the development and instruction of the unit.

> The **conceptual lens** supports a synergy between the lower levels and conceptual levels of thinking to engage the intellect (Erickson, 2008).

For example, a unit titled "Authors' Study: Three Uniquely Different Writers" might have a conceptual lens of "Authors' Craft" if the intent is to primarily focus instruction on an understanding of unique writing styles. As the works of each author in the unit are studied, the teacher would direct students' attention to the similarities and differences between the more specific (or micro) concepts that make up the idea of "Authors' Craft." The following are some further things to consider when selecting a conceptual lens for your unit:

- **The conceptual lens serves as a perceptual filter under which the more micro concepts of the unit are organized or studied.** In the above example, it provides a frame of reference for students' thinking as they examine "Authors' Craft" across different examples. Through such experiences, students begin to independently and fluidly integrate their thinking between the lower levels (factual) and conceptual levels.

- **Different conceptual lenses change the unit focus.** The unit described above would take another direction if its conceptual lens was "Perspective" and the focus was to compare the writers' messages about a topic. As you can see, a conceptual lens is a powerful tool in shaping a vision of the unit as a whole.

- **The conceptual lens is drawn from concepts that are important to the discipline.** Common conceptual lenses for English language arts are found in Table 4.1. You will notice the sample lenses (not an exclusive list!) are relevant to the discipline, will direct students' thinking and teachers' instruction throughout the unit, and will help deepen students' understanding of English language arts. A common mistake of English language arts curriculum writers is to select a lens that is more germane to another subject area, such as social studies. A lens like "Community," for example, may actually pull the focus too far away from English language arts, although it may be a great lens for an interdisciplinary unit.

Table 4.1 Sample Conceptual Lenses Used in English Language Arts Units

Relationships	Inference	Text Structure	Intent	Argumentation
Conflict	Theme	Text Features	Language	Perspectives
Characterization	Craft	Genres	Research	Patterns
Deconstruction	Process	Influence	Persuasion	Voice
Identity	Choices	Expression	Mood	Form

- **Sometimes a conceptual lens may be two words rather than one.** The lens mentioned above, "Community," may well be appropriate for an English language arts unit if another concept is connected with it. For example, "Theme/Community" brings the focus more in line with English language arts. Combining concepts to shape the unit focus can work especially well when you want the unit to get more specific (deeper) than the learning that came before (e.g., a conceptual lens of "Character" may be appropriate for a primary grade, but by the intermediate grades, the conceptual lens "Character

Relationships" works better because the study of characters within a story is more sophisticated). A dual conceptual lens also works nicely when the intent of the unit is to focus on two ideas such as "Genre/Text Structure."

- **The conceptual lens is usually decided on after examining the title and thinking about what should be the focus of the unit, but not always.** Sometimes teachers need to work through Step 3 (see Chapter 5) before the best conceptual lens emerges and is selected. Or, sometimes a lens that is selected right after the title needs to be changed as the unit develops. A final word of caution: If a concept is too narrow (e.g., "Static Character"), it is not a suitable conceptual lens. This concept would most likely be included within the unit of study, but it is too limiting to frame the study and integrate thinking. In *Concept-Based Curriculum and Instruction for the Thinking Classroom*, Erickson (2007, p. 12) provides a listing of popular conceptual lenses by subject area. Additionally, looking through the lenses used in the sample units in Chapter 5 may help trigger ideas.

SUMMARY

The unit's conceptual lens becomes a tool to think with, or to assist thinking, while exploring the content under study. Just as a camera lens is designed to magnify the subject matter and gather detail that may not be initially noticed with the naked eye, the conceptual lens for a unit provides a concept for sharpening and focusing thinking so that lower-level skills and factual knowledge (content) are interpreted at a conceptual level. Patterns across examples become more noticeable. And, as discussed previously, conceptual understanding supports the transfer of this understanding to new situations, which is our ultimate goal!

Chapter 5 delves into the process of developing the unit web. The definitions you learned for concepts will now be put into practice. The quality of the web will drive the quality of the remaining components of the curriculum unit, so patience and persistence will be required!

5 Designing the Curriculum: Step 3

Earl Nightingale's message to us all was, "We become what we *think* about." The process of writing a concept-based curriculum challenges the thinking of all involved. In the end, however, most find they approach teaching and learning very differently than they did before being introduced to this curriculum design; they become concept-based teachers who attract others striving to raise the intellectual bar.

Educators highly value thinking in students. A "thinking" or *thought-provoking* curriculum for students requires thinking teachers at the helm of both curriculum development and curriculum delivery. But it is challenging work to step back and figure out how to create a curriculum that promotes a thinking classroom.

Many professionals, just like students, become uncomfortable when new and different kinds of learning are introduced. Initial exposure to concept-based curriculum requires an understanding of new terminology, acceptance that one will be confounded at points in the process, and a realization that ongoing, deep thinking is required to effect the power of the design. This is one of the reasons why curriculum writing is such a valuable professional development experience. The thinking does not stop once the curriculum is written. The curriculum writers will feel a responsibility to convey the intellectual nature of concept-based instruction and promote classroom implementation that preserves the integrity of the design.

There is no doubt that implementation will require additional teacher professional development. A concept-based curriculum requires a pedagogical shift toward facilitating synergistic thinking and away from dispensing information. This pedagogy must be learned, practiced, and assimilated into each teacher's unique style. But before we think about implementation, we need to finish developing our units. So let's move to Step 3 in the concept-based curriculum design process for English language arts. As a template, continue to use page 43 of the form you began filling out in the previous chapter. Please note, the steps to curriculum unit writing do not always follow the exact order of the pages in the template. Reasons for this will be explained as each unit component is introduced.

STEP 3: CREATING THE UNIT WEB

The Structure of the Unit Web

The purpose of the web is to identify the potential subtopics and concepts that may be included in the unit. Completing the web is a brainstorming, prewriting exercise. This is an important initial step. Our conceptual mind is deliberately set in motion so that we first think about understandings before we consider the important facts and skills.

> **Strands** are cogent representations of the *capabilities* expected in English language arts standards.

The subtopics and concepts in the web are organized by *strands,* or cogent representations of the *capabilities* expected in English language arts standards, around the unit title and conceptual lens. Creating the unit web brings energy and focus to the design team. The strands of the web for English language arts follow:

- Understanding text
- Responding to text
- Critiquing text
- Producing text

> **Text** is defined as any media, print or nonprint, used to communicate an idea, an emotion, or information.

The use of the word *text* in each strand carries a broad meaning. *Text* is defined as any media, print or nonprint, used to communicate an idea, an emotion, or information. This is further explained in the next section where I define each strand. These strands support the integration of, and strong reciprocity among, English language arts processes. For example, the strand *understanding text* represents the *construction of meaning* whether it is *viewing* a film, *reading* print, or *listening* to a speech. The strand *producing text* incorporates the processes of *writing, speaking,* and *presenting.*

How Is Each Strand Defined?

Understanding Text

This strand represents concepts learners must understand in order to *construct meaning* from texts they are reading, hearing, or viewing. It is not enough to only comprehend at a surface level. Deeper comprehension requires conceptual understanding, thoughtful responses that reflect new connections, and the ability to critically analyze information.

> **Understanding text** represents the concepts learners must understand in order to *construct meaning* from texts they are reading, hearing, or viewing.

Responding to Text

This strand comprises the concepts readers, writers, listeners, and viewers need to understand in order to generate a quality response and to play an effective role in discourse. This is important if students are going to be moved beyond responses such as "I liked this book" or "It is really awesome" or "This is boring."

Responding to text supports, among other things, the development of the following:

> **Responding to text** comprises the concepts readers, writers, listeners, and viewers need to understand in order to generate a quality response and to play an effective role in discourse.

• **Collaboration.** 21st century skills emphasize collaboration in a diverse world. In order for students to collaborate, they need to learn how to adapt their communication and reactions in relation to audience, task, and purpose. *Responding to text* supports personal connections and reactions to text but also opens the mind to the thinking of others. A response brings out how text might clash with, change, or confirm one's views. Evidence from text is cited to substantiate the response. As students consider another person's response, they often come to appreciate nuances they never noticed initially. *Responding to text* is a strand that helps students realize how seeking out responses from others and being engaged and open-minded in their thinking and interactions will deepen their learning.

• **Exchange of Ideas.** Responding is not only about just sharing one's opinion or feelings, as mentioned above. We know that social exchanges can enhance one's thinking and deepen understanding. To make sure the discourse is meaningful requires an understanding of the concepts behind the practice of responding. When we provide opportunities for students to respond to text, we initially ask them to explain the effect the text or content under study had on them. As students share and discuss their responses to text, they may begin to hear ideas they did not pick up on and may examine a fresh perspective. In today's diverse classrooms, the exchange of ideas broadens the understanding of cultural viewpoints in the context of responding.

• **Personal Connections.** "Personal connections" is often a concept that is listed under this strand. Students need to understand the concept of "connection" if they are going to create meaningful connections that will deepen comprehension (Lanning, 2009). Again, the concepts will grow in sophistication through the grades.

Other examples of concepts in this strand include the following:

- Discussion protocols
- Reflection
- Background knowledge
- Synthesis of ideas
- Responsibility
- Participation
- Feedback
- Focus
- Clarification
- Explanation
- Questions

Responding to text strengthens and supports *understanding text*, and vice versa.

Critiquing Text

Although one could make the case that *critiquing text* is actually a subset of *responding to text*, it is separated for a reason. In the past, secondary teachers tended to overemphasize critiquing text. A work would be deconstructed and analyzed for weeks at the expense of students being able to bring their personal response into the conversation. The opposite was more typical for elementary teachers. Students would have opportunities to say why they liked or disliked books and how they made connections with text, but there was very little critiquing going on! The Common Core State Standards are rife with expectations about close reading—deep analysis throughout all the grade levels. I can only hope this is not interpreted as teachers reverting back to firing questions at students about the content of the book! "Who was Mary?" What did she grow in her garden?" "What color were the flowers?"

> Critiquing text identifies concepts readers and listeners need to understand in order to be *discerning* about text.

The web strand *critiquing text* identifies concepts readers and listeners need to understand in order to be *discerning* about text. The Common Core State Standards stress the importance of capabilities such as comparing multiple texts, judging the information in a graphic, and questioning an author's and a speaker's assumptions. An understanding of concepts brings relevance to these complex skills. Critiquing texts also offers the opportunity to develop an appreciation of an author's craft. *Understanding* the value of critiquing and all that it entails prepares students to be better consumers of the information in the world.

Producing Text

The strand *producing text* addresses concepts important to the production or generation of text. Producing may take the form of a speech, a presentation, a visual, multimedia, or writing. Understanding the concepts behind the key content, processes, strategies, and skills that go into the production of text supports the transfer of learning to a new situation. For example, the broad concept of "voice" may be relevant to a unit of study. Depending on the grade level, some micro concepts or ideas that can be unpacked from the broader concept of "voice" and may appear under the web strand *producing text* include:

> **Producing text** addresses concepts important to the production or generation of text. Producing may take the form of a speech, a presentation, a visual, multimedia, or writing.

Feelings/emotions	Vocabulary
Audience awareness	Authenticity
Individual/personal	Style
Font choice	Mood
Tone	Direct/indirect voice

Why These Strands?

The suggested strands were selected because they promote instructional integration and emphasize the *desired results* of a comprehensive English language arts curriculum versus a means to the end. Rather than separating out the communication processes of reading, writing, speaking, listening, viewing, and presenting into discrete strands around the web, the four suggested strands, *understanding text, producing text, responding to text, and critiquing text,* represent a more integrated, comprehensive, balanced approach to literacy learning. This approach is also encouraged by the Common Core State Standards:

> Although the Standards are divided into Reading, Writing, Speaking and Listening, and Language strands for conceptual clarity, the processes of communication are closely connected, as reflected throughout this document. (Common Core State Standards Initiative, 2010, p. 4)

These four web strands collectively encourage the use of multiple and varied text resources. Text should be more the "vehicle" for practicing the desired competencies in English language arts rather than the major focal point. We teach the reader and the writer, not the book and the piece! It is the *processes* required in English language arts that we want to develop fully so that students can transfer them flexibly across multiple texts and different types of text.

To review, these strands are cogent representations of the *capabilities* expected in English language arts standards, and the word *text* in each strand is defined as any *media, print or nonprint, used to communicate an idea, an emotion, or information.*

Subtopics and Concepts

Under each strand in your unit web, you will list both **subtopics** and **concepts.** Remember the Structure of Knowledge and Structure of Process introduced in Chapter 2 (see Figure 2.2, page 16)? These structures are important to keep in mind, because, as you will see, subtopics and concepts in your web will be derived from both *knowledge* and *processes.*

> **Subtopics** may be specific factual information or names of resources, such as book titles, multimedia, plays, or a research process.

The *subtopics* listed under each strand may be specific factual information or names of resources, such as book titles, multimedia, plays, or a research process (e.g., Big6). The *concepts* associated with each strand are those ideas that are considered important to unit instruction, and they are drawn from two sources: content and essential processes. At this point, you may want to see what sample webs look like before learning about how to create a quality web (see Figures 5.1a, 5.1b, and 5.1c).

> The **concepts** associated with each strand are ideas that are considered important to unit instruction, and they are drawn from two sources: content and essential processes.

Web Subtopics: Where Do They Come From?

In a unit titled "Exploring the Works of Edgar Allan Poe," possible subtopics under the strand *understanding text* might include "The Raven," "The Fall of the House of Usher," the American romantic movement, and so on. In other words, factual knowledge or specific resources that are a central part of the unit are listed under strands of the web. The Common Core State Standards include some subtopics (content) that may be relevant to units. As mentioned previously, there is a limited amount of topical content included in the Common Core State Standards, but some is there. For example, in a unit titled "Finding the Facts," teachers may choose to include some foundational U.S. documents as identified in the Common Core State Standards. The titles of the selected documents would be listed in the web, and any critical topics that might be part of the study of these documents would also be recorded in the web.

Figure 5.1a Example of Grade 9 Unit Web

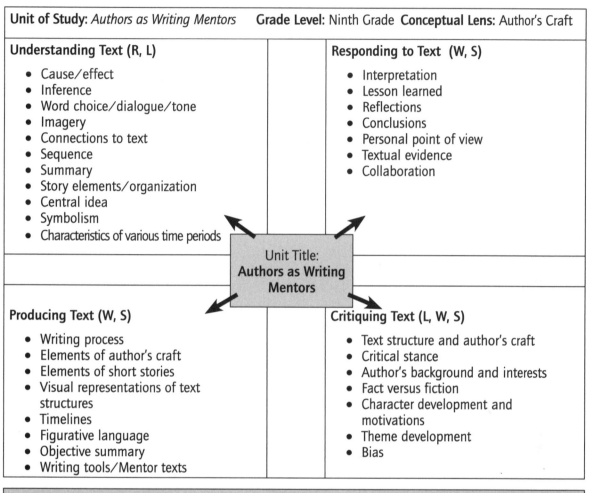

Unit of Study: *Authors as Writing Mentors* **Grade Level:** Ninth Grade **Conceptual Lens:** Author's Craft

Understanding Text (R, L)

- Cause/effect
- Inference
- Word choice/dialogue/tone
- Imagery
- Connections to text
- Sequence
- Summary
- Story elements/organization
- Central idea
- Symbolism
- Characteristics of various time periods

Responding to Text (W, S)

- Interpretation
- Lesson learned
- Reflections
- Conclusions
- Personal point of view
- Textual evidence
- Collaboration

Unit Title: Authors as Writing Mentors

Producing Text (W, S)

- Writing process
- Elements of author's craft
- Elements of short stories
- Visual representations of text structures
- Timelines
- Figurative language
- Objective summary
- Writing tools/Mentor texts

Critiquing Text (L, W, S)

- Text structure and author's craft
- Critical stance
- Author's background and interests
- Fact versus fiction
- Character development and motivations
- Theme development
- Bias

English/Language Arts Standards (Iowa Core)

RL.9-10.1. Cite strong and thorough textual evidence to support analysis of what the text says explicitly as well as inferences drawn from the text.

RL.9-10.2. Determine a theme or central idea of a text and analyze in detail its development over the course of the text, including how it emerges and is shaped and refined by specific details; provide an objective summary of the text.

RL.9-10.3. Analyze how complex characters (e.g., those with multiple or conflicting motivations) develop over the course of a text, interact with other characters, and advance the plot or develop the theme.

RL.9-10.4. Determine the meaning of words and phrases as they are used in the text, including figurative and connotative meanings; analyze the cumulative impact of specific word choices on meaning and tone (e.g., how the language evokes a sense of time and place; how it sets a formal or informal tone).

Key: R = Reading   W = Writing   L = Listening   S = Speaking

Authors: Julie Crotty, Cheryl Carruthers, Melissa Clarke, and Barb Shafer

Source: Area Education Agency 267, Cedar Falls, IA

Figure 5.1b   Sample Unit Web

Grade Level: 7

Unit Title: **Media as a Persuasive Force**

Conceptual Lens: **Persuasion/Bias**

Understanding Text:
- Nonfiction text structures and text features
- Multimedia:
  - Print media (informational), tabloids, commercial media (advertising), essay (opinion), electronic media (technology/ Internet), audio media, film, polls, slogans
- Persuasive vocabulary
- Marketing
- Political tactics

Responding to Text:
- Persuasive techniques
- Journal entries
- Group discussion
- Debate
- Privacy issues
- Public values and attitudes

Unit Title:

Media as a Persuasive Force

Producing Text:
- Types of media
- Critiques
- Persuasive writing
- Oral presentation
- Technology/media choices (for quality or effect)

Critiquing Text:
- Verbal and nonverbal language
- Persuasive techniques (e.g. imagery, word choice, sponsor)
- Validity/reliability of media message
- Social consequences of persuasive media
- Viewer responsibility
- Exploitation
- Trust

Note: In Region 15 curriculum, *text* is defined as any media, print or nonprint, used to communicate an idea, an emotion, or information.

Source: Pomperaug Regional School District 15, Middlebury/Southbury, CT

Figure 5.1c   Sample Unit Web

Grade Level: 4

Unit Title: **Realistic Fiction**

Conceptual Lens: **Genre/Features**

Understanding Text:
- Character traits
- Vocabulary
- Background knowledge
- Theme
- Author's purpose
- Text structure (rising action, climax, falling action, resolution)
- Point of view
- Self-monitor
- Inference
- Summary
- Imagery
- Narrative elements

Responding to Text:
- Connections
- Meaningful discussions
- Paraphrase
- Appeal
- Empathy

Unit Title:

Realistic Fiction

Producing Text:
- Narrative writing
- Text conventions (spelling, grammar: usage, punctuation)
- Tier vocabulary and word choice in writing
- Writing process
- Publication
- Plausible characters (details, real-life physical and personality traits)
- Dialogue

Critiquing Text:
- Author's craft (how the story "works," believability of character portrayal, etc.)
- Opinions and support
- Similarities and differences across authors, genres

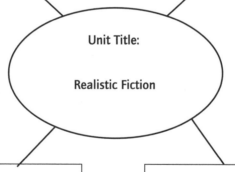

Authors: Alicia Adinolfi, Clintonville School; Kristin Buley, Montowese School; Laura Donie, Green Acres School; Mike Annino, Ridge Road School; Marie Santore and Laura Gilson, Literacy Leaders

Source: North Haven Public Schools, North Haven, CT

Web Concepts: Where Do They Come From?

In an English language arts curriculum there are usually many more *concepts* included in a unit web than subtopics. Concepts for a unit web are drawn primarily from two places:

- **Knowledge** (content) concepts that will be studied in the unit (represented by Erickson's [2008] Structure of Knowledge)
- **Process** concepts that will be focused on in the unit (represented by the Structure of Process)

Examples of concepts that might be drawn from each of these places are represented in Figure 5.2.

Figure 5.2 Concepts in Knowledge and Process

Concepts in Topic or Content Knowledge	**Concepts in Comprehension** Process	**Concepts in Production** Process
• Power • Identity • Inner conflict • Relationships • Love • Loss • Greed • Sacrifice • Choice	• Inference • Summary • Connections • Imagery • Background knowledge • Self-regulation • Purpose • Critical analysis	• Voice (tone, mood, dialect) • Audience • Text structure • Conventions • Text features • Story elements • Literary techniques • Genres

Note: Text is defined as any media, print or nonprint, used to communicate an idea, an emotion, or information

Source: "Structure of Knowledge" from *Stirring the Head, Heart, and Soul: Redefining Curriculum, Instruction, and Concept-Based Learning,* third edition, by H. L. Erickson, 2008, Thousand Oaks, CA: Corwin. Reprinted with permission.

Concepts drawn from content (knowledge) will be supported by factual examples (evidence directly from text) and are typically listed in the web beneath the strand *understanding text.*

Let's look more closely at the concepts that might be drawn from unit content. To decide on these concepts, teachers need to discuss the important ideas within the unit's topic and materials. If you return to the example of a unit titled "Exploring the Works of Edgar Allan Poe," *concepts* for this unit might include guilt, obsession, depression, and evil. These concepts would be listed below the strand *understanding text* because they are ideas that are key to comprehending the texts that will be included in this unit.

Concepts drawn from process come from several sources. Initially, web concepts may come from thinking across the strands of the web with the unit's conceptual lens in mind. For example, the fourth-grade unit titled "Finding the Facts" might have a conceptual lens of "research" as a focus for the unit. The curriculum writing team uses the lens as a frame to identify the more specific concepts to include in the web. Let's consider some possibilities of concepts that might appear under each strand in this unit:

Understanding text: Main idea, task definition, relevant information, search process

Responding to text: Questions, paraphrase, feedback, reflection

Critiquing text: Evaluation (of process and product), source authenticity, validation

Producing text: Sources, synthesis, format, writing conventions (e.g., quotations, citations)

Concepts drawn from process also come from thinking more deeply about the English language arts expectations for the unit. You will notice in Figure 5.2 that the concepts in process fall into two major categories: comprehension and production. These categories represent the two essential areas of a process-based discipline such as English language arts. Concepts from these categories continue to be drawn out and appointed across the four strands of the web from the curriculum writers' discussions about the unit content and the processes students must use to think and learn.

> The Common Core State Standards for English Language Arts are another source for process concepts.

The Common Core State Standards for English Language Arts are another source for process concepts. Closely reading through the Common Core State Standards for English Language Arts at each grade level, concepts begin to emerge. My suggestion is to use a highlighter to mark the concepts (macro and micro) you locate within each standard.

For example, in the Common Core State Standards, Anchor Standard 4 for reading states:

Interpret words and phrases as they are used in a text, including determining technical, connotative, and figurative meanings, and analyze how specific word choices shape meaning or tone. (Common Core State Standards Initiative, 2010, p. 10)

Table 5.1 shows the concepts mentioned within this standard for literature from kindergarten through Grade 12.

Table 5.1

Grade Level	Sample Concepts Aligned With Standard
K	Unknown words
1	Sensory words, emotion words
2	Regular beats, alliteration, rhyme, repetition
3	Literal language, nonliteral language
4	Allusion
5	Figurative language, metaphors, similes
6	Figurative meaning, connotative meaning, word choice, tone
7	Figurative meaning, connotative meaning, sound devices
8	Figurative meaning, connotative meaning, word choice, tone, analogies, allusions
9–10	Figurative meaning, connotative meaning, cumulative impact, word choice, time, place, formal tone, informal tone
11–12	Figurative meaning, connotative meaning, word choice, multiple meanings

When adding process concepts to the curriculum unit web, the concepts should represent greater specificity as the grade levels increase. For example, in the Common Core standard depicted in Table 5.1, teachers would want to unpack the more micro (specific) concepts behind the macro (broader) concept of "figurative meaning" to show a progression or increasing depth of understanding through the grade levels. More sophisticated readers understand concepts such as "metaphorical," "idiomatic," and "ironic," so these concepts would begin to show up in the higher grades under the web strand *understanding text.* This is why it is important to work in small, collaborative teams of curriculum writers. The collective wisdom and teaching expertise of the team flushes out the more finite concepts much more readily than a teacher can do working alone.

The more micro (specific) the concept is, the more expertise it takes to understand it. In other words, the curriculum units will build depth of understanding as concepts become more exact. If only broad, macro concepts are repeated in K–12, then we are back to a curriculum that is focused on breadth, not depth. In kindergarten, understanding the concept of "character" is a big idea and an important concept in understanding text. By the secondary grade levels, students demonstrate a greater depth of understanding about this

> The more micro (specific) the concept is, the more expertise it takes to understand it.

Figure 5.3 Micro Concepts

Drawing out micro concepts in web strand: Understanding Text (Content Knowledge)	Drawing out micro-process concepts in web strand: Producing Text	Drawing out micro-process concepts in web strands: Understanding Text (Process) Responding to Text (Process)
Character: • Main character • Protagonist • Antagonist • Hero • Antihero • Persona • Three-dimensional • Flat • Dynamic • Static	Voice: • Feelings/emotions • Audience awareness • Individual/personal • Font choice • Vocabulary • Authentic • Style • Mood • Tone • Direct/indirect	Connections: • Imagery/ visualization • Prior knowledge/ experience • Predictions • Text comparisons • Patterns • Synthesis of ideas • Relationships • Questions

(macro) concept as they talk about "static characters," "protagonists," "antagonists," "dynamic characters," "round characters," and the like.

Concepts in English language arts come from *process, strategies, and skills* as depicted in the Structure of Process (see Figure 2.2, p. 16). Again, the implication here is that in order to increase depth of understanding through the grade levels, often the macro concepts in a broader process need to be drilled down to the more specific, micro concepts that represent the important strategies or skills that support understanding the process. An example here would be that in kindergarten students learn that text needs to make sense (comprehension process). As students become more proficient readers, the more micro concepts drawn from strategies that support the comprehension process, such as inference, summary, connections, and self-regulation (Lanning, 2009), become part of the unit web. Figure 5.3 shows the relationship between macro and micro concepts. As understanding of more micro concepts grows, so does the expertise of the learner.

Concepts represent the transferable ideas relevant to each of the web strands and thus provide the assurance that the curriculum unit will support deep understanding of the important aims of English language arts. Looking through the sample webs will help bring clarity to designing a quality unit web.

SUMMARY

The collaborative brainstorming required to create the unit web can bring energy and focus to the design team. A major goal of creating a unit web is to find the relevant ideas of the unit of study prior to making decisions about other curriculum components such as factual content, key skills, or assessments. The web makes the concepts of the unit visible. As curriculum writers identify the important concepts of the web, there is considerable professional discussion and reflection. The specific strands of the web call deliberate attention to the elements of an integrated and comprehensive English language arts curriculum, which helps to minimize gaps. It is amazing to see teams of teachers huddled together closely observing the progress of a web under development as they think at a conceptual level for what may be the first time in a long while.

The point is we won't get students to a conceptual level of thinking if we first aren't explicitly aware of those important concepts that serve as the building blocks of the understandings we want students to have.

There is support for the four strands of an English language arts concept-based curriculum unit web suggested in this chapter. See if you can "hear" the rationale for the four web strands, *understanding text, responding to text, critiquing text,* and *producing text,* as you read through the following section from the Common Core State Standards for English Language Arts, which offers a portrait of students who meet the standards set out in the document:

> They build on others' ideas, articulate their own ideas, and confirm they have been understood . . .
>
> They comprehend as well as critique. Students are engaged and open-minded—but discerning—readers and listeners. They work diligently to understand precisely what an author or speaker is saying, but they also question an author's or speaker's assumptions and premises and assess the veracity of claims and the soundness of reasoning.
>
> They value evidence. Students cite specific evidence when offering an oral or written interpretation of a text. They use relevant evidence when supporting their own points in writing and speaking, making their reasoning clear to the reader or listener . . .
>
> Students appreciate that the twenty-first-century classroom and workplace are settings in which people from often widely divergent cultures and who represent diverse experiences and perspectives must learn and work together. Students actively seek to understand other perspectives and cultures through reading and listening, and they are able to communicate effectively with people of varied backgrounds. (Common Core State Standards Initiative, 2010, p. 7)

Chapter 6 will explain how the concepts in the web are used to write statements of understanding, or generalizations, that students will come to understand by the end of the unit. This next step is at the heart of concept-based curriculum design.

6 Designing the Curriculum: Steps 4 and 5

In this chapter we will work through the process of writing strong generalizations and guiding questions. Most concept-based curriculum units include five to eight powerful generalizations that we want students to understand by the end of the unit. You may wish to use the segment of your planning template shown on page 45.

> Most concept-based curriculum units include five to eight powerful generalizations that we want students to understand by the end of the unit.

THINKING AND UNDERSTANDING

If understanding is a product of thinking (Perkins, 1992), then teachers need to be clear on the expected, transferable understandings that they wish students to attain from each lesson they design. Deeper understanding of complex ideas transfers at the *conceptual level,* so the role of generalizations in concept-based curriculum is to make the expected understandings *apparent to teachers.*

For example, an English language arts curriculum unit at the secondary level may include the generalization "Propaganda exerts a powerful influence on the actions and opinions of others when not consciously observed." This is the understanding that teachers want students to realize by the end of the unit of study. When planning a lesson, teachers will use this unit generalization (and the others within the unit) to help make decisions about which texts to include and the type of work to assign with the goal of leading students to this understanding.

Erickson (2008, pp. 28–32) references the work of Hilda Taba (1966) who advocated that generalizations should determine the direction and depth for instruction. Taba believed that specific content should be sampled rather than covered. The unit generalizations play a critical role in concept-based curriculum because they enable us to make informed decisions about how much content to include in a unit.

STEP 4: WRITING GENERALIZATIONS

In Chapter 2, generalizations were defined as the clear, compelling statements of understanding that will direct instruction and assessments. A generalization includes two or more concepts (selected from the unit web—this is where all that web work pays off!) stated in a relationship that uses a strong verb. Weak verbs (*affect, impact, influence, is, have, are*) are labeled no-no verbs because they result in broad surface-level statements that lack clarity and do not express the desired depth of understanding (Erickson, 2008).

> Generalizations are clear, compelling statements of understanding that will direct instruction and assessments.

Concept 1 + Strong Verb + Concept 2 = Generalization
(More Concepts Optional)

This is also a good time to review additional criteria for recognizing a quality generalization (Erickson, 2008). Generalizations are

- broad and abstract (to varying degrees);
- universal in application;
- generally timeless (they may need a qualifier if the ideas do not hold up through time in all cases);
- represented by different examples, which support the generalization; and
- two or more concepts, stated in a relationship.

When writing generalizations,

- Be sure two or more separate ideas are not being pushed together in one statement. When a generalization ends up several lines long, it becomes very confusing to understand and is a good indication there may be multiple ideas strung together.
- Make the language as cogent and precise as possible and the statement clear. Instruction in a concept-based curriculum is designed so that students independently realize the idea through inductive teaching.
- Avoid proper nouns, or pronouns, in generalizations and use no past-tense and/or future-tense verbs (so that the generalization is transferable through time and situations).

- Avoid passive voice. A helpful remedy is to flip the sentence from passive voice to active voice. For example, "The moral of the fable was revealed by the characters' interactions" (passive voice) becomes "Characters' interactions reveal the moral of a fable" (active voice). The reordering makes the idea more precise and clear.
- Avoid overusing qualifiers. As mentioned in the definition above, sometimes a qualifier (*may, often, can, frequently,* etc.) is necessary because although the generalization is important to the unit study, it but may not hold true across all situations. Beware of falling into the trap of overusing qualifiers, however!
- Finally, do not write a generalization that reflects a value statement. Beliefs and values are not universal.

Assessing Your Prior Knowledge

Here is a little assessment of your understanding of generalizations. This "quiz" is inserted to help correct any misunderstandings and to provide feedback that may help you as you continue to learn more about generalizations. See how you do before continuing on in the chapter! The answers are on page 79.

Quiz: Do the following statements represent strong, quality English language arts curriculum generalizations? Why or why not?

1. Research helps historical fiction writers authentically portray the time period and characters of their story.

2. A well-informed citizen should read widely.

3. Grammar and sentence construction affect the clarity of a writer's message.

4. Argument may transform attitudes by breaking down intolerance.

5. Authors use stories and pictures to share their experiences and ideas.

Now we are ready to examine some of the finer points of writing generalizations that support "quality control" of the work.

Kick-Starting Generalization Writing

In Chapter 2, Erickson's (2008) structure for writing quality generalizations was introduced. She suggests starting with the sentence stem "Students will understand that . . ." This stem is then later dropped off when the generalization is written in the curriculum unit. This sentence starter launches the crafting of a generalization statement so that it reflects an important, transferable understanding. Table 6.1 lists sample generalizations that represent both process (comprehension and production) and knowledge.

Table 6.1 Sample Generalizations

Generalization *By the end of the unit, students will understand that . . .*	*Represents understanding of . . .*
1. Hard choices in life can make people stronger.	Knowledge (from text)
2. Poetry often calls upon readers to utilize background knowledge and inference to discover meaning.	Comprehension Process
3. Poetic devices (metaphors, personification, alliteration, similes, onomatopoeia) help convey a message and ignite a reader's emotions and imagination.	Production Process

Aligning Generalizations to the Unit Web

Generalizations frame the learning experiences teachers will develop when implementing the unit. Because generalizations play such a central role in concept-based curriculum and instruction, the unit generalizations, as a whole, need to address all the strands of the web to provide assurance that the unit represents a comprehensive, balanced literacy curriculum.

As curriculum writers, you will now review the concepts identified in the unit web and begin to consider relationships among them. You will begin by brainstorming some of the generalizations that students will be expected to derive throughout this unit of study. As concepts are joined to make statements of transferable understanding—generalizations—they become the rationale for studying the unit topic and provide *relevance* to the facts and skills.

Sometimes generalizations are written to articulate important ideas of individual strands of the web. At other times generalizations may represent ideas that are important to multiple strands of the English language arts unit web. The reciprocity among English language arts processes encourages this interplay. This is further explained in Table 6.2 from a short stories unit.

In Table 6.2, the generalizations support teaching to these transferable understandings across different processes. Let's examine the first generalization:

Table 6.2 Sample Generalizations From a Grade 6 Short Stories Unit

1. A realistic fiction short story usually delves deeply into one incident or experience from life. *(Understanding text, producing text, responding to text)*
2. Short stories often follow a tight story line with a few central character(s) involved in swift rising action and an abrupt ending. *(Critiquing text, understanding text, producing text)*
3. The style of short story writing requires readers to make quick and accurate inferences and personal connections within a short amount of text. *(Understanding text, responding to text)*
4. Short story themes reflect individuals caught in a struggle within themselves, with another character or with the world around them. *(Understanding text, critiquing text, producing text)*
5. Short story authors carefully craft language to concisely convey a message through the use of symbolism and figurative language. *(Understanding text, producing text, critiquing text)*

Source: Pomperaug Regional School District 15, Middlebury/Southbury, CT

A realistic fiction short story usually delves deeply into one incident or experience from life.

1. Think about the various lessons the teacher might develop when teaching toward this generalization that would support students' *comprehension* of how short stories are constructed (*understanding text*).

2. Think about how the generalization will also guide lessons about writing short stories (*producing text*).

3. Consider *questions* the teacher might pose around this generalization along with opportunities for students to share and discuss their responses to texts (*responding to text*).

The learning experiences should be designed to nudge students' thinking so they arrive at the conclusion "A realistic fiction short story usually delves deeply into one incident or experience from life." When students have many occasions (across text examples and across learning situations) to discover the generalization, conceptual patterns begin to emerge, and the transferable idea (generalization) begins to be realized.

These aha moments are what we live for in teaching and are what make learning memorable to students.

Generalizations represent different levels of abstractness, generalizability, and complexity. When students first encounter new learning, the conceptual load of the generalization will be more limited. For example, the generalization *"People* write to share a *message* with a *reader"* is a simple statement of conceptual relationship that would be appropriate for kindergarten students. The understanding grows in sophistication as more concepts are added in the next grade level, making the generalization more specific. *"Punctuation, capitalization,* and *interesting words* help make *writing* clear and appealing to a *reader."* How specific or broad a generalization should be is in part driven by developmental appropriateness.

The level of sophistication is also determined by the strength of the verb representing the relationship among the concepts in the generalization. Remember the no-no verbs (*affect, impact, influence, is, have, are*)? The use of a verb from this no-no list typically results in a lower-level, or Level 1, generalization. Often Level 1 generalizations are the product of trying to capture an idea during the brainstorming phase of writing generalizations. This is fine because once the idea is drafted, there is a method for moving the generalization to a more sophisticated level. The method is scaffolding.

Avoid these verbs, which create weak generalizations:

- affect
- impact
- influence
- is
- have
- are

Scaffolding Generalizations

Erickson (2008) devised a few simple questions to bring lower-level generalizations to more complex levels of thinking. For example, after brainstorming generalizations for a curriculum unit, the team of teachers noticed several were written using no-no verbs. These Level 1 generalizations are fixed by asking, "How?" or "Why?" As teachers discuss possible answers to the question, new concepts are heard in the answer. Try it! The weak, no-no verb is changed to a stronger verb as more precise concepts are added to the generalization. This revision process makes the statement grow in sophistication and clarity. Here is an example:

> **Level 1 Generalization:** A character's conflicts influence the message of a story.
>
> **Scaffolding Questions:** *How* do a character's conflicts influence the message of a story?
>
> **Level 2 Generalization:** A character's internal and external conflicts imply a deeper message about life or human nature.

Most concept-based curriculum units include five to eight powerful generalizations that we want students to understand by the end of the unit. Almost all of those generalizations will be Level 2; however, the unit may include a couple of Level 3 generalizations. How do we take an idea to Level 3? Again, Erickson (2008) suggests we answer a simple question to trigger our thinking. To move a generalization from Level 2 to Level 3, ask, "So what is the significance (or effect)?"

Below, I extend the example from above to create a Level 3 generalization:

> **Level 1 Generalization:** A character's conflicts influence the message of a story.
>
> **Scaffolding Question:** *How* do a character's conflicts influence the message of a story?
>
> **Level 2 Generalization:** A character's internal and external conflicts may imply a deeper message about life or human nature.
>
> **Scaffolding Question:** *So what?*
>
> **Level 3 Generalization:** Writers layer a character's personality to sharpen the contrast between internal and external conflict.

You may have noticed that when the generalization was moved to Level 3, it became a *new idea* that explained the significance of the Level 2 generalization. As curriculum writers, you may come up with as many Level 3 generalizations as there are people in your group because each person's mind goes to a different place in thinking about the significance of the Level 2 idea. Answering the "So what?" question takes thinking "out of the box." Coming to consensus on a great Level 3 generalization is the fun part.

Teaching With Generalizations

When you begin teaching units based on generalizations, it is worth remembering several things:

- If the generalization is declared by the teacher at the beginning of the lesson (deductive teaching), the opportunity is lost for students to think, arrive at a conclusion, and ultimately express their personal understanding.
- Although the students' conclusions or assertions may not be stated in exactly the same language as the curriculum generalization, the idea is typically explained in similar terms.
- Students may also arrive at generalizations that were not identified in the unit plan but are valid. These are indicators that you have conceptually minded students, so applaud your concept-based teaching!

Summary of Step 4

It takes practice to write generalization statements that express the powerful, transferable ideas we want students to understand by the end of the curriculum unit. Initially, writing generalizations is challenging for teachers because we are not often pushed to think at the conceptual level. The return is well worth the effort, however. Learning to extrapolate transferable understandings from content and process and to express ideas with precise language brings clarity to instruction. Generalizations make the goals of student understanding visible to teachers.

In the beginning, students also find the expectation to articulate a generalization challenging. Curriculum and instruction have a long history of focusing on the facts and skills with little emphasis on conceptual thinking. As a result, students spend most of their energy searching for "the right answer" (that is already in the teacher's head) for the assignment at hand. They become afraid to take risks and be "wrong." Concept-based curriculum and instruction teaches both teachers and students how to use a thinking process to reach a conceptual level of understanding. As students begin to realize the ideas represented by their classroom learning experiences, they may offer generalizations (and validate them with specific evidence, of course) that are not listed in the curriculum unit. This is truly something to celebrate!

Scaffolding techniques serve as quality controls when writing generalizations. With the effort and resources expended in developing a curriculum, you want assurance that the final product represents and supports excellence! Scaffolding is also a way to differentiate instruction for students who demonstrate they are ready for the more challenging thinking required in a Level 3 version of the generalization. We are now ready to move on to Step 5.

STEP 5: WRITING GUIDING QUESTIONS

After the unit generalizations are written, it is time to plan the questioning path that will be used to guide students' thinking to discover the generalizations. Guiding questions are written for *each* unit generalization. Through inquiry-based, inductive teaching, we keep pressing students closer to constructing their understanding of the idea (generalization) through various lesson examples, modeling, and questioning.

> Guiding questions are written for *each* unit generalization.

"Only a small percentage of teaching-learning experiences include explicit attention to the strategic dimension," Perkins (2009 p. 139) tells us. Discovering and explaining the hidden understandings (generalizations) behind facts, processes, assignments, and so on is not a practice common in all classrooms.

Strategic questioning is an important instructional technique used in concept-based instruction. Most of us in education were not taught about the importance of different types of questions and when to use them in our teaching. Including a range of guiding questions in the curriculum unit serves not only as an instructional resource but also as a springboard for additional questions teachers might generate.

Erickson (2007, 2008) explains questioning in the teaching-learning process. In a concept-based curriculum, guiding questions create the bridge between learning experiences and deeper understandings. Questions help students notice patterns in knowledge.

> Guiding questions create the bridge between learning experiences and deeper understandings.

Questions are motivational tools because they promote active, intellectual engagement on the part of the learner rather than the simple regurgitation of presented information. Guiding questions are written for each unit generalization for a specific reason. By aligning questions with generalizations, the questions are targeted at the generalization under study. Big, broad

> Questions help students notice patterns in knowledge.

questions may take students' minds off in many different directions. Good guiding questions keep the thinking and discussions focused.

To do this well, Erickson (2007, 2008) explains, we must understand how to distinguish among question types (factual, conceptual, and provocative). *All three* types are critical to a concept-based unit. Here is an example of questions that might be written to unpack a generalization from an English language arts unit:

Generalization: Unique traits distinguish one character from another.

Factual Questions:

- Factual questions are important to ensure the foundation of knowledge is in place.
- Factual knowledge provides the evidence for explaining understanding.

Factual questions for the generalization above might include:

What are character traits?

How does the author of your book communicate the main character's traits?

In the story "Cinderella," what are some examples of the traits of the different characters?

Conceptual Questions:

- Open-ended, conceptual questions challenge students' thinking beyond the facts.
- The response to a conceptual question will reflect an *understanding that is transferable* across situations and examples.
- Conceptual questions are similar to generalizations: There can be no proper nouns, no past-tense or passive verbs, no pronouns, and so on.

Conceptual questions for the generalization above might include:

How does an author make characters believable?

How do character traits help readers identify with characters?

How do character traits help readers better understand the story?

Provocative Questions:

- Provocative questions provoke great debates.
- There are no right or wrong answers, but these questions keep learning interesting and push thinking outside of the box as students listen to each other's perspectives.
- A unit may have two to four provocative questions but not so many that there is not time for rich discussion.

A provocative question for the generalization above might include:

How do you think the story would be different if Cinderella's character traits were changed? (Notice that proper nouns and pronouns may be used in a provocative question although this doesn't have to be the case.)

The strategic use of these questions helps ensure instruction is not overwhelming the learner with too much too fast. Jean Shoemaker and Larry Lewin (1993, p. 55) describe the role of questions in concept-based teaching like this:

> Such questions are posted in the classroom for the duration of the unit to provide structure for the unit and create clear linkages between the day-to-day activities and the major concepts. Further, in requiring students to pursue answers, the questions call upon students to produce, rather than just consume, knowledge. And, as individuals construct meaning and answers to questions, they naturally come to understand the subjective nature of knowledge.
>
> Students demonstrate their conceptual understanding by constructing personally meaningful yet plausible answers to the key questions. The answers may be expressed in a variety of forms, including personal interviews, the creation of graphic representations (such as models and concept maps), the generation of metaphorical images, and of course written essay tests.

A sample page of generalizations and guiding questions can be found in Table 6.3. This example will help you better understand the role of guiding questions in a concept-based unit.

Table 6.3 Sample Generalizations and Guiding Questions From a Concept-Based English Language Arts Unit

Grade Level: 3 Unit Title: Whodunit? Reading and Solving Mysteries	
Generalizations	*Guiding Questions* *(F = factual; C = conceptual; P = provocative)*
1. Authors use clues to build suspense or solve a problem in a mystery.	1a. Which clues helped lead you to predicting a solution? (F) 1b. How did the setting affect the mood of your mystery? (F) 1c. How do authors build suspense? (C) 1d. Why are clues important in solving a mystery? (C) 1e. Can you have mystery without suspense? (P)
2. Readers identify and connect clues to solve a mystery.	2a. What is an inference? (F) 2b. How do readers identify clues? (C) 2c. How does a prediction differ from an inference? (C) 2d. How do readers connect clues throughout a text? What happens when they don't? (C)

(Continued)

(Continued)

3. Readers gather relevant information from the text to confirm or revise predictions.	3a. What is relevant information? (F) 3b. How do readers separate relevant from irrelevant information? (C) 3c. Why is it important to revise predictions? (C)
4. Respectful consideration for the ideas of others can provide new insights and extend thinking.	4a. What does respectful conversation look like/sound like? (F) 4b. What happens when the ideas of others are not respected? (C) 4c. Do we always have to accept the ideas of others? (P) 4d. How can consideration of another person's ideas help you solve problems? (P)
5. Mysteries share common elements yet also include unique characteristics.	5a. What are the elements of mystery? (F) 5b. How are the characteristics of the mystery you are reading similar to and different from those of other mysteries? (F) 5c. Why are mysteries so popular? (P) 5d. Why are solutions so satisfying? (P)
6. Characters within a mystery may include suspect, detective, sleuth, sidekick, witness, investigator, villain, victim, criminal, or accomplice.	6a. How do you define suspect? Detective? Sleuth (etc.)? (F) 6b. Which characters are essential to your mystery? Why? (F) 6c. How do different characters contribute to a mystery? (C)

Authors: Mary Blair, Middle Gate School; Lynn Holcomb, Hawley School; Becky Virgalla, Sandy Hook School; and Eileen Tabasko, Head O'Meadow School

Source: Newtown Public Schools, Newtown, CT

Summary of Step 5

Strategic questioning means more than pulling questions out of our back pocket on the spot. Curriculum writers think through the types of guiding questions that will best support inductive teaching toward the generalization. Spending time to strategically develop examples of the three different types of questions within the unit provides teachers with suggestions for activating and guiding students' thinking. If we are not deliberate about the distinctions among different types of guiding questions, problems may occur. One problem is that the questions posed during instruction become overly fact-based and all about text or procedures. Another problem occurs when all the questions we pose to students are conceptual in our fervor to emphasize conceptual understanding. The problem here is that students need to know some factual information in order to cite specific evidence of their conceptual understanding.

Guiding questions are not a script to follow in a rote fashion. Guiding questions provide teachers with a means to advance students' thinking about ideas that lead to understanding. Questioning is a powerful instructional technique. When students' thinking is made more public, teachers can better assess whether or not students are on their way to realizing important generalizations. Balancing the types of guiding questions helps uncover misconceptions as well as extend students' thinking.

> Guiding questions are not a script to follow in a rote fashion.

In Chapter 7, the next steps of unit development are explained: identifying the critical content that students are expected to know and key skills that students are expected to be able to demonstrate by the end of the unit.

> How did you do?

Answers to Generalization Quiz (see page 69)

1. Yes, this is an excellent generalization. It is a clear and important statement that transfers across all historical fiction writing. When fifth-grade students arrive at this generalization as a result of their learning experiences and teacher modeling and questioning, they will better comprehend and appreciate how the genre is constructed. Students will also utilize this understanding as they critique works of historical fiction currently and in the future.

2. No, this is not a quality generalization. Why? It is a value statement. Although we may believe this and want it to be true, it does not qualify as an appropriate generalization.

3. No, this does not represent a strong generalization because it uses the no-no verb *affect.* Later in this chapter you will learn how to fix this problem.

4. Yes, we support this as a quality generalization! The idea is important, and the qualifier *may* represents the recognition that it may not be true across all situations.

5. Another yes! The statement is an important understanding at the kindergarten level and is written in a manner that represents grade-appropriate language.

7 Designing the Curriculum: Steps 6 and 7

S teps 6 and 7 in unit development include two additional nonnegotiable components of a quality concept-based curriculum—*critical content* (what students will know) and *key skills* (what students will be able to do).

Although facts and skills were the primary drivers of curriculum and instruction for many years, it is a mistake to think that they are now ignored in concept-based curriculum design. The beauty of concept-based design is that when curriculum writers have reached this phase of the process, they have already thought long and hard about the *conceptual understandings* (generalizations) students are expected to discover by the end of the unit. When the first priority is to clearly articulate expectations for conceptual understanding, informed decisions can be made about identifying the critical *content* and key *skills* in the unit of study.

> Critical content is what students will know.

> Key skills are what students will be able to do.

As you read this chapter, you may wish to use the segment of your planning template shown on page 46.

STEP 6: DETERMINING CRITICAL CONTENT

In Step 6, the curriculum writing team thinks about what students must *know* by the end of the unit. What students need to *know* is defined as the important, factual content (or knowledge) relative to the unit of study. A review of all the components of the curriculum up to this point (the unit title, the web, and the generalizations) provides a solid springboard for identifying the critical knowledge of the unit.

Here are several considerations that will help guide you:

> What students need to know is the important, factual content (or knowledge) relative to the unit of study.

1. **The critical content section of the unit will naturally include some of the subtopics and concepts listed in the web.** For example, in a unit titled "The Many Works of Shakespeare," the critical content teachers may want students *to know* by the end of the unit are the names of some specific works that were listed as subtopics in the unit web, such as *The Tempest, Romeo and Juliet,* and *Hamlet.*

2. **Critical content drawn from the web might include vocabulary specific to a particular genre under study.** In an elementary unit titled "Crime Solver: Understanding the Elements of a Mystery," critical content drawn from the web might include vocabulary specific to mystery books such as *suspect, victim, detective, red herring,* and so on. Although these terms were included in the unit web as concepts, the students need *to know* the factual definitions before they can think of them as abstract organizers for different characters in a mystery.

3. **Consider specific vocabulary students will need to understand and use as evidence of their conceptual understanding.** For example, consider the generalization "Writers select a voice appropriate to audience." Students would need *to know* the meaning of voice, tone, and mood. They would also need *to know* how tone is different from mood and how audiences vary in expectations. This factual knowledge is necessary if they are going to understand, be able to explain, and provide examples of the idea represented by the generalization.

Although it is not imperative, I recommend critical content be identified under each of the four strands in the web (*understanding text, responding to text, critiquing text,* and *producing text*) to help ensure nothing is missed and the unit is balanced across the important strands of English language arts. An example of this method can be found in Figure 7.1.

A note of caution: A frequent mistake when attempting to list critical content knowledge is to write more generalizations. Critical content only needs to be bulleted out, as you can see in Figure 7.1. Sometimes, in our quest to do a job right, we have a tendency to make things harder than they need to be!

Figure 7.1 Critical Content Organized by Strands

Critical Content
Students will know . . .

Understanding Text:

- Text structures of memoirs
- Author's purpose
- Key vocabulary (show, don't tell; tug at the heart; look back; vignette)

Responding to Text:

- Reader connections
- Group discourse behaviors
- Meaning of personal reflections
- Qualities of reader response

Critiquing Text:

- Author's craft (word choice, literary devices, sentence fluency)
- Author's purpose
- Text structure
- Meaning and criteria of critical stance

Producing Text:

- Process for idea generation
- Writing process
- Meaning of sentence fluency
- Different types of sentence structures
- Writing conventions
- Meaning of "transformation" (tug at the heart)
- Peer conference protocols
- Specific writing techniques (word choice, dialogue, sensory details, literary devices, sentence fluency)

Source: Grade 6 English Language Arts Curriculum, Memoir Unit, Newtown Public Schools, Newtown, CT.

STEP 7: DETERMINING KEY SKILLS

Although this section of the curriculum unit is considered the "skills" section, I have some hesitancy in using this term. The hesitation with using the term *skill* is that it is often used to describe any act whether it requires higher-level abstraction or routine recall. In this book, consider key skills as all those processes, strategies, and skills (ranging in levels of abstraction) that provide the means for understanding and using language as creative and purposeful expression.

> Key skills are those processes, strategies, and skills (ranging in levels of abstraction) that provide the means for understanding and using language as creative and purposeful expression.

Another note of caution: The key skills listed in this component of the curriculum unit should not describe in detail every finite skill students will be expected to demonstrate.

The Common Core State Standards identify, by grade level, what students must be able to demonstrate in order to be prepared for the literacy demands of college and careers in the 21st century. Those expectations, or the expectations of other standards you must meet, and those that curriculum writers determine are important to the unit of study, make up the key skills of the unit.

Grade-level standards of the Common Core are a big help here. The standards often integrate multiple lower-level skills into more rigorous and complex competencies. For example, the Grade 4 Common Core Reading (CCR) Standard for Literature 9 states

> Compare and contrast the treatment of similar themes and topics (e.g., opposition of good and evil) and patterns of events (e.g., the quest) in stories, myths, and traditional literature from different cultures. (Common Core State Standards Initiative, 2010, p. 12)

Wow! Do you see all the separate skills that are embedded in this one standard? To list them all would result in a document considerably larger than the current, concise Common Core. The standards are written this way, in part, to encourage integrated skill instruction. The document begins by explaining how the standards are organized:

> Students advancing through the grades are expected to meet each year's grade-specific standards, retain or further develop skills and understandings mastered in preceding grades, and work steadily toward meeting the more general expectations described by the CCR standards. (Common Core State Standards Initiative, 2010, p. 4)

This spiral organization makes the Common Core State Standards extremely useful to curriculum writers. Previously, state standards for English language arts often repeated skill expectations verbatim across grade levels, making it difficult for curriculum writers to decipher how skills increased in complexity from one grade level to the next. All teachers responsible for meeting the Common Core State Standards should be familiar with the document as a whole so they can see the expected *progression* in the development of competencies.

As your grade-level curriculum writing team makes decisions about the key skills that need to be addressed in each unit, the Common Core State Standards can provide a clear map to guide the work. There is no point in reinventing language when the descriptions of skills can be "lifted" directly from this document.

In Figure 7.2 you will find an example of the key skills included in a Grade 6 curriculum unit.

Figure 7.2   Key Skills Organized by Strands

Key Skills
Understanding Text:
CC.6.R.L.2
• Key Ideas and Details: Determine a theme or central idea of a text and how it is conveyed through particular details; provide a summary of the text distinct from personal opinions or judgments.
CC.6.R.L.3
• Key Ideas and Details: Describe how a particular story's or drama's plot unfolds in a series of episodes as well as how the characters respond or change as the plot moves toward a resolution.
CC.6.R.L.6
• Craft and Structure: Explain how an author develops the point of view of the narrator or speaker in a text.
Responding to Text:
CC.6.R.L.1
• Key Ideas and Details: Cite textual evidence to support analysis of what the text says explicitly as well as inferences drawn from the text.
CC.6.SL.1
• Comprehension and Collaboration: Engage effectively in a range of collaborative discussions (one-on-one, in groups, and teacher-led) with diverse partners on Grade 6 topics, texts, and issues, building on others' ideas and expressing their own clearly.

(Continued)

(Continued)

CC.6.SL.1.a

- Comprehension and Collaboration: Come to discussions prepared, having read or studied required material; explicitly draw on that preparation by referring to evidence on the topic, text, or issue to probe and reflect on ideas under discussion.

CC.6.SL.1.b

- Comprehension and Collaboration: Follow rules for collegial discussions, set specific goals and deadlines, and define individual roles as needed.

CC.6.SL.1.c

- Comprehension and Collaboration: Pose and respond to specific questions with elaboration and detail by making comments that contribute to the topic, text, or issue under discussion.

CC.6.SL.1.d

- Comprehension and Collaboration: Review the key ideas expressed and demonstrate understanding of multiple perspectives through reflection and paraphrasing.

Critiquing Text:

CC.6.R.L.5

- Craft and Structure: Analyze how a particular sentence, chapter, scene, or stanza fits into the overall structure of a text and contributes to the development of the theme, setting, or plot.

CC.6.R.L.4

- Craft and Structure: Determine the meaning of words and phrases as they are used in a text, including figurative and connotative meanings; analyze the impact of a specific word choice on meaning and tone.

Producing Text:

CC.6.L.3.a

- Knowledge of Language: Choose language that expresses ideas precisely and concisely, recognizing and eliminating wordiness and redundancy.

CC.6.L.3.b

- Knowledge of Language: Maintain consistency in style and tone.

CC.6.L.5

- Vocabulary Acquisition and Use: Demonstrate understanding of figurative language, word relationships, and nuances in word meanings.

CC.6.W.4

- Production and Distribution of Writing: Produce clear and coherent writing in which the development, organization, and style are appropriate to task, purpose, and audience.

CC.6.W.5

- Production and Distribution of Writing: With some guidance and support from peers and adults, develop and strengthen writing as needed by planning, revising, editing, rewriting, or trying a new approach.

CC.6.W.2

- Demonstrate command of the conventions of standard English capitalization, punctuation, and spelling when writing.
- A. Use punctuation (commas, parentheses, dashes) to set off nonrestrictive elements.
- B. Spell correctly.

CC.6.W.3

- Use knowledge of language and its conventions when writing, speaking, reading, or listening.
- A. Vary sentence patterns for meaning, reader/listener interest, and style.
- B. Maintain consistency in style and tone.

Source: Grade 6 English Language Arts Curriculum, Memoir Unit, Newtown Public Schools, Newtown, CT.

As you can see in the example in Figure 7.2, the key skills are again identified by the strands of the unit web. Not all districts insist on this format; however, I believe it is a valuable way to make sure some dimensions of English language arts are not given short shrift. The more "quality control" checkpoints included in the curriculum writing process, the stronger the end product will be.

It is also important for curriculum writers to remember that the standards articulate end-of-the-school-year expectations. Decisions need to be made about how to distribute standards across units where there is a "best fit" for the time of year and with the unit content under study. At the same time, some standards may need to be included in every unit of the grade level. *A note of caution:* The Common Core State Standards identify many of the capabilities students are expected to demonstrate on their path to meeting the criteria of a literate individual prepared for college and careers. The curriculum unit of study, however, may move somewhat beyond all that is listed in the standards. For this reason, it is important to have the expertise of district teachers around the table when writing curriculum. The Common Core document addresses this point:

> While the Standards focus on what is most essential, they do not describe all that can or should be taught. A great deal is left to the discretion of teachers and curriculum developers. The aim of the Standards is to articulate the fundamentals, not to set out an exhaustive list or a set of restrictions that limits what can be taught beyond what is specified herein. (Common Core State Standards Initiative, 2010, p. 6)

Additionally, the document makes it clear that it does not include the *learning support* students may need in order to meet the standards:

> The Standards set grade-specific standards but do not define the intervention methods or materials necessary to support students who are well below or well above grade-level expectations. No set of grade-specific standards can fully reflect the great variety in abilities, needs, learning rates, and achievement levels of students in any given classroom. However, the Standards do provide clear signposts along the way to the goal of college and career readiness for all students. (Common Core State Standards Initiative, 2010, p. 6)

Curriculum writers may sometimes consider deconstructing those standards that are more complex and require high levels of abstraction. Having this information broken down and spelled out in the curriculum unit helps teachers know how to best address students who are lagging behind in their literacy learning. For example, in *Four Powerful Comprehension Strategies for Struggling Readers* (Lanning, 2009), the comprehension process is broken down into four strategies that all proficient readers use. Each of these essential comprehension strategies requires time and mental effort to achieve as texts build in sophistication and complexity. Capable readers figure this out, but students who struggle with reading comprehension do not. The book lists many of the skills that are the underpinnings of the four comprehension strategies and that struggling students need to realize tie directly to the more abstract strategy. Adding this information to the unit (or referencing the professional resource) may help teachers become more aware of the skills that support essential comprehension strategies (without overdoing it as discussed previously).

Drawing on the work of David Perkins and others, *Four Powerful Comprehension Strategies* (Lanning, 2009) also explains how struggling students become overwhelmed when instruction assumes they can achieve *far transfer* of learning. Far transfer refers to the attempt to transfer learning from one context to another when the sense of connection between the two learning situations requires deeper thinking, knowledge, understanding, and careful analysis. For example, the strategy of "inferring" demands a high level of abstraction. Instruction that focuses on understanding the concept of *inference* and all that a reader must think about and *do* (skills) while inferring provides the support necessary to advance transfer and sustain students' reading progress toward the required standards.

Not all competencies listed in the curriculum unit will represent higher-level thinking requiring conceptual understanding and transfer. Many skills are practiced with such frequency in language arts classes, and the tasks are so perceptually similar from one learning situation to the next, that transfer is not an issue. For example, skills such as capitalizing proper nouns, identifying the main character of a story, using commas in greeting and closing of letters, and reading decodable words with automaticity become routine through regular practice, and transfer is typically not problematic. These skills do not require a high level of abstraction, and the task is very consistent in nature from one situation or text to the next.

SUMMARY OF STEPS 6 AND 7

All Common Core State Standards listed in the curriculum unit's key skills section need to be directly taught and practiced. Some standards, however, are more sophisticated and, especially as text gets more complex, require a higher level of abstraction and conscious cognitive processing. In order to support transfer, instruction needs to make sure all students understand the foundational skills and *concepts* within the standards so that, "as students advance through the grades and master the standards in reading, writing, speaking, listening, and language, they are able to exhibit with increasing fullness and regularity these capacities of the literate individual" (Common Core State Standards Initiative, 2010, p. 7).

A Quick Review of Things to Avoid

1. **When listing key skills in the curriculum unit, do not write about the learning experiences or lesson activities that will lead to those skills.** Sometimes curriculum writers erroneously include learning experiences in the competency component of the curriculum. For example, "Students will complete a graphic organizer showing the sequence of events in the story 'Cinderella.'" This is an activity, not

a skill. Completing a graphic organizer may be the vehicle the teacher uses to teach the skill of "sequencing events in a story," but learning experiences are included in another section of the curriculum unit. Skills are written so they are tied neither to a specific text (or topic) nor to an instructional activity because they need to transfer across many applications and contexts.

2. **Do not allow the key skills identified in the curriculum unit to become an exhaustive list of discrete bits of skills.** Curriculum writers need to be selective about how much detail to add to standards that need "unpacking," or the document quickly becomes unwieldy and impractical for teachers. Often a solution is to list the titles of learning resources that will further explain and provide instructional support for some of the more complex standards. An example here is the Common Core Language Standard 2 (Grades K–12), "Demonstrate command of the conventions of standard English capitalization, punctuation, and spelling when writing" (Common Core State Standards Initiative, 2010, pp. 26, 28, 52, 54). Rather than list the breakdown of all the stated and implied skills in this standard, the curriculum unit may instead reference a district resource that is aligned with the expectations of the standard (e.g., "Demonstrate the *Words Their Way* spelling competencies expected in Grade 4").

3. **Do not write more generalizations when attempting to list critical content knowledge.** Remember, critical content simply needs to be bulleted out.

Chapter 8 moves the curriculum writing process to the end of the unit before returning to finish the parts in the middle. The unit now has a strong framework to help direct the design of the culminating task students will complete to demonstrate all they understand, know, and are able to do as a result of the instruction of this unit.

8 Designing the Curriculum: Steps 8, 9, and 10

At this point in writing a concept-based curriculum unit, assessment becomes the focus. A quality, end-of-unit assessment provides the evidence teachers need to be confident that students have attained the expected understandings, knowledge, and key skills by the end of the unit of study.

Step 8 entails designing the culminating assessment. In Step 9 we consider how to pace and structure lessons to prepare students for the end-of-unit task. Finally, in Step 10, our work is to write an engaging unit overview that will guide teachers as they introduce the unit to their students.

For Steps 8 and 9, you may wish to use the portions of the planning template shown on pages 48, 47, and 43, respectively.

STEP 8: DESIGNING
THE CULMINATING ASSESSMENT

Writing a quality assessment takes thought and collaboration. The Common Core State Standards offer suggestions for performance assessment tasks. They support designing instruction and assessments that integrate multiple standards so that tasks do not become overly limited and decontextualized:

> Often, several standards can be addressed by a single rich task. For example, when editing writing, students address Writing standard

5 ("Develop and strengthen writing as needed by planning, revising, editing, rewriting, or trying a new approach") as well as Language standards 1–3 (which deal with conventions of standard English and knowledge of language). When drawing evidence from literary and informational texts per Writing standard 9, students are also demonstrating their comprehension skill in relation to specific standards in Reading. When discussing something they have read or written, students are also demonstrating their speaking and listening skills. The CCR anchor standards themselves provide another source of focus and coherence. (Common Core State Standards Initiative, 2010, p. 5)

Once again, Erickson (2008) provides us with a smart structure that helps keep curriculum writers on the path of writing a quality assessment. "A major problem with many performance tasks is that there is too often little or no display of deep understanding. I think this is once again because our traditional curriculum design only takes us to the superficial level of topics and facts" (Erickson, 2008, p. 98). Follow her recommended structure in Figure 8.1, and the culminating task for the unit will assess deep understanding.

Figure 8.1a   Model for Writing a Unit Culminating Performance Task

WHAT: Begin this statement with a cognitive verb such as *investigate* and tie it directly to the title of your unit.

WHY: . . . in order to understand that . . .

Complete this statement by thinking beyond the title to the importance or significance of the study. What is important is to identify a generalization (understanding) you want students to be able to demonstrate as a result of this unit of study. This generalization is tied directly to the culmintating performance task.

HOW: Begin a new sentence that frames and outlines how you want students to demonstrate their understanding of the "why" statement. This is a critical step. If you want to measure deep understanding, then the "how" needs to demonstrate the "why" and not just demonstrate knowledge of the facts or skills learned in the "what" statement. In describing the task, Erickson suggests picking up language from the generalization (identified in the step above) as a way of ensuring the generalization is being addressed.

Figure 8.1b   Blank Culminating Performance Task

WHAT: Investigate . . . (unit title or major topic)

_____

_____

_____

_____

_____

_____

WHY: In order to understand that . . . (enduring understandings)

_____

_____

_____

_____

_____

_____

HOW: (Performance)

_____

_____

_____

_____

_____

_____

_____

_____

Source: From _Stirring the Head, Heart, and Soul: Redefining Curriculum, Instruction, and Concept-Based Learning_, Third Edition (p. 99), by H. L. Erickson, 2008, Thousand Oaks, CA: Corwin. Reprinted with permission.

The example below follows Erickson's (2008) assessment template and represents a culminating task for an English language arts unit titled "Language as a Tool of Power."

> **WHAT:** Investigate the power that language can wield . . .
>
> **WHY:** . . . in order to understand that language skills may inhibit or strengthen the ability to control the fate of oneself or others.
>
> **HOW:** In this unit we read many different fiction and nonfiction texts that revealed the power of language. Consider the texts you have read throughout the unit and the article (distributed in class) that showed how the number of corporations owning the majority of U.S. media outlets went from 50 to 5 from 1993 to 2004. Take a stance on how you see this significant decline in who controls the language of media as either a positive situation or cause for concern. In your paper, cite specific examples from your readings that support your position.

Do you see how this task will show whether or not students arrived at the understanding represented in the generalization noted in the "why" statement? Do you also see the other knowledge and competencies that are assessed by this task? A rubric used as a scoring guide for this task would include criteria that reflect students' depth of understanding as well as their progress toward other standards addressed in the unit. There are numerous resources available online for developing rubrics and other types of scoring guides.

A note of caution here is to make sure that the criteria for understanding are not missing from the scoring guide! It is important to write scoring guides with precise language describing the expected quality. Too often scoring guide language is vague or written in negative terms—what is not evidenced in student work versus what is. This is not helpful to students or clear to the teachers who are doing the scoring.

> A note of caution here is to make sure that the criteria for understanding are not missing from the scoring guide!

Here are some final thoughts on writing the culminating unit task:

1. **Consider whether or not there is an overarching generalization for the unit.** If there is, it becomes the focus in the final task. Sometimes curriculum writers use the last generalization of the unit in the culminating performance task, or it may be that two unit generalizations (no more or it will be too much) are combined. These are decisions that curriculum writers need to make after considering the unit as a whole.

2. **Remember that the culminating assessment is not the only time students' learning progress is considered.** Throughout the unit, teachers will use many different types of assessments (response, essay, observations, performance, self-assessments, etc.) to closely monitor and provide feedback on students' learning. You will see in the next component of the concept-based unit, Step 9, how some ongoing assessment ideas are suggested to teachers.

3. **Culminating assessment tasks vary considerably in the scope of student work required.** A culminating assessment task that requires students to complete research prior to writing a final summary may take many weeks to complete. Students are learning about the research process as they are working collaboratively with peers on components of the assessment task. Other culminating assessments may be completed in a much shorter time period. What is important is that the final student product that is graded by the teacher must be completed by each student independently.

Do you see why it is important for curriculum writers to be clear about the expected understandings, knowledge, and skills in the unit prior to writing the end-of-unit assessment? If the culminating task is written too quickly, it may not represent the most important elements of the unit of study.

What We Can Learn From Culminating Assessments

The culminating unit task becomes a common assessment across all classrooms that participated in the unit of study. When grade-level teachers gather together to share and analyze their students' results from a common task, the result is inevitably a very rich professional discussion about student work and instructional methods and, consequently, a powerful professional development experience. Not only does the sharing reflect a genuine professional learning community, where peer collaboration supports all teachers and students; it is additionally a valuable way to evaluate the curriculum. For example, if student confusions become evident across over 80% of the classrooms, it is most likely a curriculum issue. If student performance is uneven across classrooms, it is more likely an instructional issue, and the collective wisdom of colleagues can help. Paying attention to the results of the culminating task also supports fidelity to curriculum implementation.

STEP 9: SUGGESTING LEARNING EXPERIENCES

Now we are ready for the section that everyone loves. This step in unit writing occurs *after* the development of the culminating assessment because this section offers suggestions for how to pace and structure lessons that will *prepare* students for the end-of-unit task. The big decision for curriculum writers is to figure out *how much* information to suggest.

A note of caution: This section of the unit is not about writing teachers' lesson plans.

A note of caution: This section of the unit is not about writing teachers' lesson plans.

There are several purposes for this section:

- **To communicate some of your district's instructional practices** (guided reading, workshop model, cooperative learning, etc.). Offering examples of learning experiences that represent expected curriculum implementation practices helps teachers make the connections as they design their own lesson plans.
- **To offer suggestions for pacing the learning experiences so that students across classrooms are prepared for the culminating task within a similar time frame**. Pacing may be broadly suggested—for example, learning experiences to launch or introduce the unit, learning experiences midway through the unit, and learning experiences to implement toward the end of the unit. Suggested learning experiences might also be organized by weeks. The grade-level team of curriculum writers knows teachers in their district best and how much guidance will be helpful without becoming overly prescriptive.
- **To support transfer success.** Remember, this is one of the most important goals of a concept-based curriculum. How the learning experiences are structured and delivered has a strong influence on whether or not the goals of a concept-based curriculum are achieved. Teachers are very familiar with instructional methods that require drill and practice. These methods work fine for those processes that involve a consistent application of skills performed more or less the same way and in a similar context each time (near transfer). As this book has argued in past chapters, to accomplish *far* transfer of more complex, abstract learning, instruction needs to go beyond and teach for understanding. Teachers appreciate suggestions for designing these types of learning experiences.

Although there is no one method to teaching for far transfer, the learning experiences usually begin with brief, mini-lessons where teachers model and describe the metacognitive processes used in a specific part of a task. These "exemplars" often help students reflect on their thinking as they continue their work.

Suggested learning experiences should involve a degree of problem solving and judgment in situations (or texts) that are different each time. When students are asked to compare and contrast authors' styles, for example, they begin to derive generalities (generalizations) from the specific instances. Tasks that require deep processing, such as analyzing analogies, developing an argument for a particular position after reading multiple viewpoints, developing a counterargument, and so on, help students to construct mental models of understanding as they grapple with the work. These examples are in sharp contrast to lessons that tell students, "Here is what you are going to learn," "Here is how you do it," and, finally, "Now, go do it." This type of lesson may help build the procedural, near-transfer skills but will not build the mental models (previous knowledge) students need to retrieve when trying to make sense of new knowledge. Many of the literacy demands today require people to select relevant information from the massive amount available, organize it, integrate it with prior knowledge, and carefully critique it before making decisions. The intent of the Common Core State Standards is to prepare students for these expectations, so the majority of the suggested curriculum unit learning experiences must reflect work that builds students' conceptual thinking.

David Perkins (2009) sees a "pothole" that shows up in the design of many lessons intended to teach toward understanding.

> The pothole we see . . . shows up in many other activities that we might think of as good understanding performances: write an essay, write a story, produce a diagram, develop a discussion, create a dramatization, and so on. All these are promising because they offer ample *opportunity* for understanding performances. However, they do not typically *require* extensive on-target thinking. (pp. 66–67)

This takes us back to the point that an ample number of the suggested learning experiences must be designed so that students *truly demonstrate understanding.* Students may be required to complete the work examples described by Perkins (2009), but if they are not pushed beyond to *reflect* on the process, integrate knowledge, *explain* the choices made, and articulate the idea represented by the product, the learning experience falls short of our curriculum goal.

- **To communicate a clear and direct link back to the generalizations, critical content, and key skills that students must be able to demonstrate by the end of the unit**. Learning experiences that address the content and skills are usually straightforward. Learning experiences that are designed to guide students' thinking to the unit generalizations are not always as apparent to teachers. As a result, curriculum writers often code the suggestions to specific unit generalizations.

Here is an example:
A suggested *learning experience* might be:

After student partners review the criteria for evaluating a quality PowerPoint presentation and the methods for creating one, have them discuss how and why they will use this information to structure their individual class presentations. (G#2)

The code, G#2, refers to the second *generalization* in the unit, which states:

An audience's understanding of a speaker's point of view depends on the style, accuracy, clarity, and pacing of the presentation.

This cross-referencing of generalizations to learning experiences helps keep the goal of the understanding—the transferable idea—in the forefront of instruction versus focusing only on the presentation skills or content knowledge required in the learning experience. The various learning experiences and the teachers' guiding questions lead students to realize the generalization over the course of the unit.

Other information that is pertinent to teachers' lesson planning may be tagged to the suggested learning experiences. In the example in Figure 8.2, curriculum writers designed a template that describes learning experiences but also offers suggestions for during-unit assessments, potential differentiation ideas, and resources that could assist with instruction.

Some districts require that the Common Core—or other standards—be coded to learning experiences. (Other districts require that the Common Core State Standards addressed in the unit be documented on a separate page.) Working with grade-level colleagues who know what will be most useful for a successful curriculum implementation should drive your decision making.

Summary of Steps 8 and 9

The learning experiences provide teachers implementing the curriculum with suggestions for planning their instruction of the unit and preparing

Figure 8.2 An Excerpt of Suggested Learning Experiences From a Grade 3 Folklore and Fantasy Unit

Suggested Timeline	Suggested Learning Experiences (The teacher may . . .)	Assessments (Suggested and Required**)	Differentiation (For Support and Extension)	Teacher and Student Resources
Week 1	Suggested teaching points in **reading** and **writing workshop** mini-lessons: Each day introduce and read aloud different folktales using various guiding questions and ask students to discuss what they are noticing about the characteristics of a folktale. Maintain a "master" chart of responses to the following questions for each folktale: **(G#1)** • Where is the setting of this tale? • Who are the characters? • Who is the folktale written for? • What is the author's purpose? • Is there a theme/message of the folktale? **(G#5)** **Provide ongoing instruction/modeling of suggested teaching points in both reading and writing instruction.** Teacher models strategies and skills readers use to infer theme or message (using text evidence and background knowledge)	Observation, students' (oral, written, assigned task) responses Assess the text evidence students provide to support their responses See if students notice patterns across the folktale chart—Are they discovering **G#1**? Assess students' applications of teaching points in assigned tasks beyond the mini-lesson** Notice whether or not students are using text language/vocabulary when responding in small/large group discussions and in writing Assess the text evidence students provide to support their oral and written responses**	Reference to classroom charts (routines, how to check work, etc.) Answer frames as needed Independent reading of additional, longer-length folktales Small group or individual guided instruction	Mentor text: *Anansi the Spider* series Provide a variety of folktales for students to read and use with work assigned after mini-lesson

(Continued)

99

(Continued)

| Week 2 | Model how to problem solve challenging vocabulary words utilizing context clues

Students explore questions while revisiting familiar folktales and new: What is an idiom? How do idioms convey the message or moral of a folktale? (G#1)

Students explore questions while revisiting familiar folktales:

- How do the illustrations help a reader understand the character's traits or feelings? (G#1)
- How do illustrations help to convey the theme or message?
- How do illustrations depict the culture of the folktale? (G#3)

In small and whole group student-led discussions, ask students to formulate opinions about the quality of the illustrations and text features in a familiar folktale utilizing text evidence and learning. (G#3) | Assess students' *understanding* as they make their thinking visible (through explanation and examples)

Assess the text evidence students provide to support their responses

Assess students' *understanding* as they make their thinking visible (through explanation and examples)

Evaluate student recommendations/ presentations

Provide ongoing monitoring of individual writing journals that assigned tasks relative to teaching points | Preteach vocabulary words

Continue with ideas above

Guide students' thinking by cueing as needed

Utilize support from library media specialist or other specialist teachers | Mentor text: *The Lion and the Mouse*

Continue to provide a variety of folktales for students to read and use with work assigned after mini-lesson |
|---|---|---|---|---|

Week 3		Students' written or oral reflections	Character trait word bank	Mentor text: *Why Mosquitoes Buzz in People's Ears*
	How does an author's choice of character help convey the meaning or message of the text? **(G#1)** Using the text _____, how would you describe the character? Make sure you provide evidence to support your thinking. **(G#1)** Ask student partners to critically analyze characters and events in a text and be prepared to recommend or not recommend the folktale: • Was the story engaging? Why or why not? • Did the author accomplish his or her purpose? Why or why not? • Is the story's message relevant to everyone or just some? Why or why not? (Etc.) **(G#1, 3, 4, 5)** Which character are you most like? Why? How does this affect your opinion of the story? **(G#4)** Which folktale most connects to your own experiences? **(G#5)** **Continued . . .**		Use sticky notes or highlighting to locate information One-on-one teacher modeling with more explicit instruction	Continue to provide a variety of folktales for students to read and use with work assigned after mini-lesson

Key: G = Generalization

Source: North Haven Public Schools, North Haven, CT. Authors: Janice Regan, Grade 3, Green Acres School; Marylyn Tantorski, Grade 3, Ridge Road School; Corki Cuomo, Grade 3, Montowese School; Marilyn Sapienza, K–5 Language Arts Consultant, Montowese School.

students for the expectations of the unit's culminating assessment. The unit's suggested learning experiences are merely that—suggestions for how to best design unit lessons. The assessments used throughout implementation of the unit will provide specific feedback to teachers regarding additional learning experiences students need.

The learning experiences offered in the unit of study should be logically sequenced and incrementally more demanding, and reflect the quality instructional techniques valued by the district. You do not want to undo concept-based curriculum with learning experiences that revert to mindless worksheets or activities that students merely complete but that do not guide students' conceptual thinking! There is certainly a place for explicit instruction of skills and content; however, learning experiences can be structured so that student work requires thinking, questioning, dialoguing, noticing patterns, connecting, and critically analyzing. Doing so ensures students will be on their way to transferable, conceptual understanding.

Finally, the nature of the culminating assessment determines the number of learning experiences to suggest for a unit. Sometimes, as mentioned previously, the assessment task takes several weeks of work prior to students' completion of a final, independent piece. All these considerations are taken into account by the curriculum writers as they map out unit learning experiences.

STEP 10: WRITING THE UNIT OVERVIEW

Congratulations! You have arrived at the final step in the process of writing a concept-based curriculum unit. This step entails writing an overview that gives teachers language to introduce the unit to their students. Are there any intriguing questions that might be asked to pique students' interest in the learning that lies ahead? Is there a short scenario that might be read aloud that would capture students' attention? Is there any background knowledge that might be tapped to interest students? These are just a few of the options that curriculum writers might use. Below are two examples of a unit overview:

> Who is your hero? Do all heroes have to be real? What makes a hero a hero? In our next unit, we will travel back in time through the literature of the peoples who lived in Britain in the early Middle Ages—Britons, Anglo-Saxons, Vikings, and Normans. We will explore the literature, history, religion, and language of these cultures, and focus on representations of the heroic ideal, as embodied

in mythic, legendary, and historical writing. We also will consider the traits of the heroes of the early Middle Ages and see how they compare with those you consider present-day heroes. You may be surprised at the similarities and differences!

I need information! My friend and I are planning a trip for our school vacation, and we are not sure where we should go. We only have six weeks to figure this out. We want to go somewhere warm; we both love to swim; we want to make sure it is not too far away because I only have a week. Finally, it can't be too expensive! Hmmm . . . where do I begin finding all the information I need? Well, in our new unit, I am going to show you the research process I use to find the right information so I can pick the perfect vacation spot. The best part is that after we all return from vacation, I am going to write about the place I visited, using the information I collected before I left as well as my experiences there. This could be a helpful guide for someone else, don't you think? We will experience the research process together—I will be doing my research while you research information about a topic you would like to learn more about. You will also write about what you learned and share it with our class. We have lots to do, so let's get started!

Summary of Step 10

Writing a unit overview is the grand finale of unit writing. Customizing the description of the unit so that students are intrigued about the work ahead gets the unit off to a great start. Although the unit overview conveys the content focus of the unit, the questions and narrative descriptions are a way to capture the students' hearts and minds on Day 1.

Chapter 9 includes a few sample units from different districts and grade levels. Looking over these units as a whole will help you see how all the components of concept-based curriculum complement each other and leverage teaching and learning.

Part III

What a Concept-Based Curriculum Looks Like

9 What Concept-Based English Language Arts Units Look Like

One mission of this book is to support readers' understandings of concept-based curriculum design. Let's try another little assessment to check on how well I am accomplishing this mission. Try writing two generalizations that capture your understandings of concept-based curriculum now that you have reached this point in the book. Keep in mind the criteria for writing a powerful generalization.

How did you do? Below is a sample generalization that may capture the idea in one of your responses:

Readers will understand that . . .

A conceptual curriculum serves as a guide to meeting high standards.

In an excellent 2007 mathematics article, writers Rina Zazkis, Peter Liljedahl, and Egan J. Chernoff share the essential role that examples play in a student's ability to form and refute generalizations. They assert that the instructional examples to which students are exposed play a critical role in developing their ability to arrive at a generalization. As discussed in previous chapters, exposing learners to numerous examples of an understanding you are teaching toward helps them begin to notice patterns and move their thinking from the specific examples to a conceptual level of understanding. This is the synergistic thinking that will help them better retain their learning and transfer it to new situations (Erickson,

2008). Additionally, Zazkis et al. (2007) discuss the role of pivotal examples. Pivotal examples are specifically selected to either create or resolve some cognitive conflict and cause the learners to change their mind or abandon original thinking. In other words, the choice of examples can help promote successful generalizations or refute incorrect generalizations.

The length restrictions of this book do not allow for a large number of unit examples. Some districts that have moved to designing concept-based curriculum acknowledge the power of examples and make their units available for a nominal fee to help support others who are new to the process (e.g., Pomperaug Regional School District 15 of Middlebury and Southbury, Connecticut). This chapter showcases three examples of units that have some subtle nuances in their designs but maintain fidelity to a conceptual approach. Hopefully these examples and the others scattered throughout the book promote a successful understanding of the concept-based curriculum design process.

A SAMPLE ELEMENTARY ENGLISH LANGUAGE ARTS UNIT

Let's begin by looking at a Grade 2 unit from North Haven Public Schools in North Haven, Connecticut.

The web section of Figure 9.1 shows the initial brainstorming efforts that went into planning the concepts that provide the foundation for the unit. Notice the web does not include key skills! Those appear later in the unit and also in the suggested learning experiences. The generalizations are balanced across all strands of the web, so they represent understandings important to comprehensive, balanced literacy learning. What is also interesting about this unit is that teachers organized their suggested learning experiences around each unit generalization. Notice that the teachers writing this unit presented the suggested learning experiences so that they would fit nicely into the reader's and writer's workshop framework they use for lesson planning.

(Text continued on page 121)

Figure 9.1 Sample Elementary Concept-Based English Language Arts Unit

K–12 English Language Arts Curriculum

Grade: 2

Title: Character Study: How do we get to know characters?

Date: January 26, 2012

Grade Level: 2

Unit Title: **Character Study: How do we get to know characters?**

Conceptual Lens: **Characterization**

Understanding Text:
- Major events and challenges
- Story elements of narrative text
- Characters' points of view
- Characters' traits, dialogue, actions
- Characters' voice
- Vocabulary
- Qualities of friendship
- Summary
- Grade-level phonics and word analysis
- Inference
- Questions to support comprehension
- Fluency

Responding to Text:
- Meaningful connections to characters
- Text evidence
- Partner read/share
- Similarities and differences of characters across texts
- Key ideas and details
- Comprehensive descriptions

Unit Title:

Character Study: How do we get to know characters?

Producing Text:
- Oral/written responses (to literal, interpretive, and open-ended questions)
- Shared writing
- Narrative writing
- Writing conventions
- Writing process
- Temporal words
- Transition words
- Eye contact, speaking voice
- Opinion pieces (writing journals)

Critiquing Text:
- Opinions of author's depiction of characters supported by text evidence
- Believability of character
- Realistic problem/solution
- Quality of text illustrations
- Conclusions

Grade Level: 2

Unit Title: Character Study: How do we get to know characters?

Conceptual Lens: Characterization

Unit Overview (an engaging summary to introduce students to the unit work)
  Mini-lesson format
  Now that you have reached second grade, I know that you have read and written many stories. One of the key elements of a story is the characters. How do authors help you become acquainted with characters? How do you form an opinion about whether or not you like a character, believe the character could be real, or think you or someone you know could be just like the character in a story? We are going to figure out some of the answers to these questions as we work through this new unit. By the end, not only will you be able to add more details to the characters in your stories, but in our new books, you may also discover some characters who feel like old friends!

Connecticut Common Core State Standards addressed in this unit:
Common Core State Standards included in this unit are identified in the key skills section.

Grade Level: 2
Unit Title: Character Study: How do we get to know characters?

Generalizations	Guiding Questions (F = factual; C = conceptual; P = provocative)
1. Character dialogue and actions reveal character traits.	1a. What are character traits? (F) 1b. What is story dialogue? (F) 1c. How do writers let readers know when characters are "talking"? (F) 1d. How can character traits be used to describe a character? (C) 1e. What are the character traits of the main character in the story __? (F) 1f. What did the character say and do that proves these traits are accurate? (F) 1g. How does other information in text help support a reader's understanding of a character? (C) 1h. Can a character trait be both good and bad? (P)
2. Background experiences help readers identify and relate to story characters.	2a. Who are the main characters in the book _____? (F) 2b. Who are the supporting characters in the book? (F) 2c. How are main characters different from supporting characters? (C) 2d. How might characters change from the beginning to the end of a story? (C) 2e. What experiences have you had that are similar to characters in stories? (P) 2f. Do characters always change in a story? Cite evidence from different books. (F)
3. Authors develop a story and its characters based on genre and purpose.	3a. What is genre? (F) 3b. What is the genre of the story ___, and how do you know? (F) 3c. What evidence from the text __ shows you that the character is/is not believable? (F) 3d. Do all characters have to be believable? (P) 3e. What is the problem and solution in the story __? Support with text evidence. (F) 3f. How are the characters a good match (or not) for a story? (C) 3g. How do authors pick characters for stories? (C) 3h. What does the voice of the character ___ sound like? (F)
4. Character relationships shape and drive events in a story.	4a. What is a relationship? (F) 4b. What are different types of relationships? (F) 4c. How can relationships change over time? (C) 4d. Why do relationships change? (C) 4e. What is the relationship of the characters in the story __? (F) 4f. Did the characters' relationship change throughout the story? If so, how? (F) 4g. How can changes in character relationships affect the rest of a story? Support with examples. (C) 4h. How might the outcome of the story __ change if the characters had a different relationship? (P) 4i. How do differences in characters' points of view make a story more interesting? (C)
5. Readers make inferences about characters using evidence from the text.	5a. How does the way a character acts help a reader make predictions? (C) 5b. What do good readers do when a prediction is not correct? (F) 5c. What is an inference? (F) 5d. What clues did you find in this story that led you to believe the character ___? (F) 5e. Do all clues lead to the same inference? (P) 5f. Why do inferences sometimes change? (C) 5g. What evidence led you to like or admire the character __? Why or why not? (P) 5h. How do illustrations affect a reader's inferences? (C)

Critical Content and Key Skills

Critical Content *Students will know . . .*	*Key Skills* *Students will be able to do . . .*
Understanding Text: • Story elements of narrative text • Authors write for different purposes • Vocabulary in context • Strategies (pre, during, post) for reading • Predictions create anticipation • Retell/summarize • Meaning of inference • Meaning of character traits/voice	**Understanding Text:** **CCSS RF.2.3**: Know and apply grade-level phonics and word analysis skills in decoding words. **CCSS RF.2.4**: Read with sufficient accuracy and fluency to support comprehension. **CCSS RL.2.1**: Ask and answer such questions as *who, what, where, when, why,* and *how* to demonstrate understanding of key details in text. **CCSS RL.2.3**: Describe how characters in a story respond to major events and challenges. **CCSS RL.2.6**: Acknowledge differences in the points of view of characters, including by speaking in a different voice for each character when reading aloud. **CCSS L.2.4**: Determine or clarify the meaning of unknown and multiple-meaning words and phrases based on Grade 2 reading and content, choosing flexibly from an array of strategies. **CCSS RL.2.7**: Use information gained from illustrations and words in a print or digital text to demonstrate understanding of its characters, setting, or plot.
Responding to Text: • Meaning of meaningful connections to text • Different levels of questioning/responding—literal, interpretive, and philosophical • Discussion behaviors • How to use text evidence to strengthen response	**Responding to Text:** **CCSS SL.2.1**: Participate in collaborative conversations with diverse partners about *Grade 2 topics and texts* with peers and adults in small and larger groups. **CCSS SL.2.2**: Recount or describe key ideas or details from a text read aloud or information presented orally, or through other media. **CCSS W.2.8**: Recall information from experiences or gather information from provided sources to answer a question. **CCSS L.2.6**: Use words or phrases acquired through conversations, reading and being read to, and responding to texts, including using adjectives and adverbs to describe.
Critiquing Text: • Meaning of opinion vs. fact • Elements of critiquing author's craft (believability of character, illustrations, realistic problems/solutions, etc.)	**Critiquing Text:** **CCSS RL.2.4**: Describe how words and phrases (e.g., regular beats, alliteration, rhymes, repeated lines) supply rhythm and meaning in a story, poem, or song. **CCSS RL.2.5**: Describe the overall structure of a story, including describing how the beginning introduces the story and the ending concludes the action. **CCSS W.2.1**: Write opinion pieces in which they introduce the topic or book they are writing about, state an opinion, supply reasons that support the opinion, use linking words (e.g., *because, and, also*) to connect opinion and reasons, and provide a concluding statement or section.
Producing Text: • Written response with text evidence • Narrative text structure—story elements • Stages of the writing process • Meaning of temporal and transition words • Writing conventions for Grade 2 • Oral presentation protocols	**Producing Text:** **CCSS W.2.3**: Write narratives in which they recount a well-elaborated event or short sequence of events, include details to describe actions, thoughts, and feelings, and use temporal words to signal event order, and provide a sense of closure. **CCSS L.2.2**: Demonstrate command of the conventions of standard English capitalization, punctuation, and spelling when writing.

Week 1: Suggested learning experiences to guide students to understanding that . . .
G#1: **Character dialogue and actions reveal character traits.**

Teaching Point	Guiding Questions	Suggested Resources	Assessments	Recommended Structures
• Readers notice how characters talk to each other. • Writers use specific techniques to show character dialogue. • Characters can be described by how they look, act, or feel. • Character traits are words that are used to describe how a character looks, acts, or feels. • Readers/writers identify character traits in their own reading and writing.	• What is story dialogue? (F) • What are character traits? (F) • How can you use character traits in your writing to describe a character? (C) • What are the character traits of the character(s) in the story? (F)	• *Chrysanthemum,* Mary Hoffman • *Ira Sleeps Over,* Bernard Waber • *Chester's Way,* Kevin Henkes • *Frog and Toad,* Arnold Lobel • *Tacky the Penguin,* Helen Lester • *Thank You, Mr. Falker,* Patricia Polacco • *Henry and Mudge,* Cynthia Rylant • *Officer Buckle and Gloria,* Peggy Rathmann • *Stand Tall, Molly Lou Melon,* Patty Lovell • *Skippyjon Jones,* Judy Schachner	• One-on-one conferring • Teacher observations • Students' oral/written responses	• Leveled Library • Reading/Writing Workshop • Partnerships • Read Aloud • Guided Reading • Strategy Groups • Shared Reading and Writing • One-on-One Reading and Writing Conferences

Week 2: Suggested learning experiences to guide students to understanding that . . .
G#1: Character dialogue and actions reveal character traits.

Teaching Point	Guiding Questions	Suggested Resources	Assessments	Recommended Structures
• Readers use clues that writers create in the text to figure out how a character looks, acts, and feels.	• How can you use information from the text to support your description? (C) • What did the character say that proves that he/she is _____? (F) • What does a character do that proves he/she is _____? (F) • Do all characters have traits? (F) • Could a character trait be both good and bad? (P) • How can you include clues about characters in your stories? (F)	• *The Recess Queen*, Alexis O'Neill • *Hop Jump*, Ellen Stoll Walsh • *Jamaica's Find*, Juanita Havill • *Sheila Rae, the Brave*, Kevin Henkes • *A Weekend With Wendell*, Kevin Henkes • *Odd Velvet*, Mary Whitcomb • *Chester's Way*, Kevin Henkes • *Oliver Button Is a Sissy*, Tomie dePaola	• One-on-one conferring • Teacher observations • Students' oral/ written responses	• Leveled Library • Reader's/Writer's Workshop • Partnerships • Read Aloud • Guided Reading • Strategy Groups • Shared Reading and Writing • One-on-One Reading and Writing Conferences

Week 3: Suggested learning experiences to guide students to understanding that . . .
G#2: Background experiences help readers identify and relate to story characters.

Teaching Point	Guiding Questions	Suggested Resources	Assessments	Recommended Structures
• Readers identify the main and supporting characters. • Readers and writers differentiate between the main and supporting characters.	• Who are the main characters and supporting characters? (F) • How are main characters different from supporting characters? (C)	• Texts mentioned above and . . . • Additional mentor texts • Six traits • Students reading and writing journals	• One-on-one conferring • Teacher observations • Students' oral/written responses • Evaluation of assigned work • Writing portfolios • Reading logs	• Leveled Library • Read's/Writer's Workshop • Partnerships • Read Aloud • Guided Reading • Strategy Groups • Shared Reading and Writing • One-on-One Reading and Writing Conferences

Week 4: Suggested learning experiences to guide students to understanding that . .
G#2: Background experiences help readers identify and relate to story characters.

Teaching Point	Guiding Questions	Suggested Resources	Assessments	Recommended Structures
• Readers and writers track character traits throughout the story. • Readers make connections to the characters in the story.	• How might characters change from the beginning to the end of the story? (C) • What experiences have you had that are similar to character(s) in the story? (C) • Do characters always change in a story? Cite evidence from different books. (F)	• Mentor texts • Students' writing journals • Six traits • Students' reading and writing journals	• One-on-one conferring • Teacher observations • Students' oral/written responses • Evaluation of assigned work • Writing portfolios • Reading logs	• Leveled Library • Reader's/Writer's Workshop • Partnerships • Read Aloud • Guided Reading • Strategy Groups • Shared Reading and Writing • One-on-One Reading and Writing Conferences

Week 5: Suggested learning experiences to guide students to understanding that . . .
G#3: Authors develop a story and its characters based on genre and purpose.

Teaching Point	Guiding Questions	Suggested Resources	Assessments	Recommended Structures
• Readers and writers differentiate between informational and fictional text. • Readers find clues that writers create to determine if a character is realistic.	• What is genre? (F) • What is the genre of the story and how do you know? (F) • What evidence from the text shows you the character is/is not believable? (F) • Do all characters have to be believable? (P)	• Pair-it books • Students' reading and writing journals • Six traits	• One-on-one conferring • Teacher observations • Students' oral/written responses • Evaluation of assigned work • Writing portfolios • Reading logs	• Leveled Library • Reader's/Writer's Workshop • Partnerships • Read Aloud • Guided Reading • Strategy Groups • Shared Reading and Writing • One-on-One Reading and Writing Conferences

Week 6: Suggested learning experiences to guide students to understanding that . . .
G#3: Authors develop a story and its characters based on genre and purpose.

Teaching Point	Guiding Questions	Suggested Resources	Assessments	Recommended Structures
• Readers and writers recognize different types of relationships. • Readers and writers track how relationships can change over time and what happens as a result.	• What is a relationship? (F) • What are different types of relationships? (C) • How can relationships change over time? (C) • Why do relationships change? (C)	• Reader's/writer's notebooks/journals • Six traits vocab.	• One-on-one conferring • Teacher observations • Students' oral/written responses • Evaluation of assigned work • Writing portfolios • Reading logs	• Leveled Library • Reader's/Writer's Workshop • Partnerships • Read Aloud • Guided Reading • Strategy Groups • Shared Reading and Writing • One-on-One Reading and Writing Conferences

Week 7: Suggested learning experiences to guide students to understanding that . . . .
G#4: Character relationships shape and drive events in a story.

Teaching Point	Guiding Questions	Suggested Resources	Assessments	Recommended Structures
• Readers and writers recognize different types of relationships. • Readers and writers track how relationships can change over time and what happens as a result.	• What is a relationship? (F) • What are different types of relationships? (C) • How can relationships change over time? (C) • Why do relationships change? (C)	• Reader's/writer's notebooks/journals • Six traits vocab.	• One-on-one conferring • Teacher observations • Students' oral/written responses • Evaluation of assigned work • Writing portfolios • Reading logs	• Leveled Library • Reader's/Writer's Workshop • Partnerships • Read Aloud • Guided Reading • Strategy Groups • Shared Reading and Writing • One-on-One Reading and Writing Conferences

Week 8: Suggested learning experiences to guide students to understanding that . . . .
G#4: Character relationships shape and drive events in a story.

Teaching Point	Guiding Questions	Suggested Resources	Assessments	Recommended Structures
• Readers and writers determine the relationship between characters in a story. • Readers need to notice how writers sometimes change character relationships and how the change affects the story.	• What is the relationship between the characters in the story ____? (F) • Did the characters' relationship change throughout the story? If so, how? (F) • How can changes in characters' relationships affect the rest of a story? Provide examples. (C) • How might the outcome of the story ____ change if the characters had a different relationship? (P) • How do differences in characters' points of view make a story more interesting? (C)	• Reader's/writer's notebooks/journals • Six traits	• One-on-one conferring • Teacher observations • Students' oral/written responses • Evaluation of assigned work • Writing portfolios • Reading logs	• Leveled Library • Reader's/Writer's Workshop • Partnerships • Read Aloud • Guided Reading • Strategy Groups • Shared Reading and Writing • One-on-One Reading and Writing Conferences

Week 9: Suggested learning experiences to guide students to understanding that . . .
G#5: Readers make inferences about characters using evidence from the text.

Teaching Point	Guiding Questions	Suggested Resources	Assessments	Recommended Structures
• Readers notice things that authors want us to know but don't use the words to state.	• What is an inference? (F) • What clues did you find in this story that led you to believe _____? (F) • Do all clues lead to the same inference? (P) • Why do inferences sometimes change? (C) • What evidence led you to like or dislike the character _____? Why or why not? (P)	• As above	• One-on-one conferring • Teacher observations • Students' oral/written responses	• Leveled Library • Reading Workshop • Partnerships • Read Aloud • Guided Reading • Strategy Groups • Shared Reading and Writing • One-on-One Reading and Writing Conferences

Week 10: Suggested learning experiences to guide students to understanding that . . .
G#5: Readers make inferences about characters using evidence from the text.

Teaching Point	Guiding Questions	Suggested Resources	Assessments	Recommended Structures
• Readers make predictions based on the way the character acts. • Writers provide clues to readers about characters.	• How does the way a character acts help a reader make predictions? (C) • What do good readers do when a prediction is not correct? (F)	• As listed previously	• One-on-one conferring • Teacher observations • Students' oral/written responses • Culminating unit assessment task (to be developed: presentation rubric)	• Leveled Library • Reader's/Writer's Workshop • Partnerships • Read Aloud • Guided Reading • Strategy Groups • Shared Reading and Writing • One-on-One Reading and Writing Conferences

Culminating Performance Task:

WHAT? Students will investigate the traits of a favorite character . . .

WHY? . . . in order to understand that character dialogue and actions reveal character traits.

HOW?
Step 1: Choose a character from one of the stories you have read during this unit.
Step 2: Reread the story and decide on one of the character's traits you would like to investigate.
Step 3: Complete the character trait web:

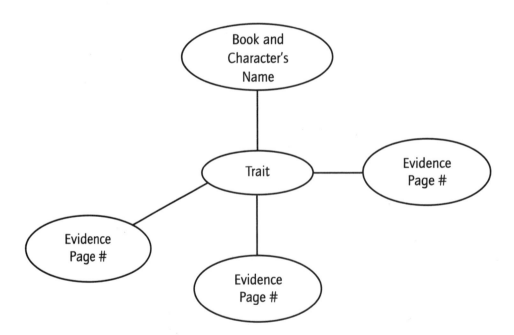

Step 4: Present your findings to the class and what you found out about how authors reveal character traits.

Authors: Josh Anderson, Marie Camerato, Jennifer Ciaburro, Carrie Gambardella, Rachel Sullivan

Source: North Haven Public Schools, North Haven, CT

(Continued)

A SAMPLE MIDDLE SCHOOL ENGLISH LANGUAGE ARTS UNIT

The next example, shown in Figure 9.2, comes from Pomperaug Regional School District 15 of Middlebury and Southbury, Connecticut. It is a Grade 6 unit written around a conceptual topic titled "How Can We Change the World?"

(Text continued on page 132)

Figure 9.2   Sample Middle School Concept-Based English Language Arts Unit

 POMPERAUG REGIONAL SCHOOL DISTRICT 15
Serving the Communities of Middlebury and Southbury, Connecticut

K–12 Language Arts Curriculum

Grade: 6

Unit 4: How Can We Change the World?

Date: January 2012

Source: This unit was published in *Pomperaug Regional School District 15* in Middlebury/Southbury, Connecticut, and can be used with permission.

If you would like to purchase this language arts unit, please call (203) 758-8259 extension 114 (Assistant Superintendent of Schools Office).

Grade Level: 6

Unit of Study: How Can We Change the World?

Conceptual Lens: Critical Stance

Understanding Text: (R, V, L)
- Cause/effect
- Voice—point of view
- Structure of nonfiction and fiction
- Content for accuracy and bias
- Social activism
- Injustice
- Inference
- Empathy
- Change in attitude

Responding to Text: (L, S, P)
- Consideration of other points of view/ flexible thinking
- Lesson learned
- Relevant questions
- Reflection
- Connections
- Summarization
- Synthesis of texts/ideas
- Personal viewpoint
- Dynamics of productive discussion

Unit Title:

How Can We Change the World?

Producing Text: (P, W, S)
- Persuasive writing techniques
- Research process
- Oral expression
- Defense

Critiquing Text: (L, V, R, S, P)
- Writer's craft—analysis of text structure/ author's reasoning
- Critical stance—justification of outcome/conclusions
- Argumentation
- Author's purpose
- Bias
- Content accuracy

Key:
R = Reading
L = Listening
V = Viewing
S = Speaking
W = Writing
P = Presenting

Note: In Region 15 curriculum, *text* is defined as any media, print or nonprint, used to communicate an idea, an emotion, or information.

Grade Level: 6

Unit of Study: How Can We Change the World?
(Time Frame: Approximately 6 Weeks)

Conceptual Lens: Critical Stance

Unit Overview (an engaging summary to introduce students to the unit work):

Have you ever had to take a stance on something you truly believed in or felt strongly about? Have you experienced an injustice and wanted to take action? You have the ability to bring about changes in your world. In this unit, we will explore authors' craft, point of view, and an author's critical stance. As a social activist, you will express and defend your own viewpoint on a controversial issue. After researching your topic, you will write a letter expressing your point of view and offering your suggestions for solving the problem.

Technology Use: (What skills do teachers or students need to use this? How much knowledge or familiarity with the use of the Internet and tools are necessary?)

Appropriate research—use of the Internet, magazines, newspapers, books.

The Region 15 English Language Arts Curriculum has been cross-checked and aligned with the Common Core State Standards

Grade Level: 6
Unit of Study: How Can We Change the World?

Enduring Understandings (generalizations)	Focus Questions (F = factual; C = conceptual; P = provocative)
1. An opinion piece (documentary film, newspaper editorial, book, etc.) can change the beliefs, convictions, and opinions of an individual or a group. (UT, RT)	1a. What is social activism? (F) 1b. Why do people read or write about social change? (C) 1c. How is your point of view formed? (F) 1d. What is the relationship between an individual and a group in creating social change? (C) 1e. What social changes have affected your life, school, town, and world in general? (F)
2. Ideas in text can evoke provocative discussions that move groups to action and result in transformative change. (UT, RT, CT)	2a. What literary techniques do writers employ to persuade? (F) 2b. What makes the subject matter relevant? (F) 2c. What literary techniques do writers employ to convey their stance on an issue? (F) 2d. What is the status quo? (F) 2e. Why challenge the status quo? (C) 2f. When is it OK to preserve the status quo? (P) 2g. What is conflict? (F) 2h. How do you interpret text when the author's position is neutral? (C)
3. Many authors create conflict in text through word choice, voice, and subject matter to challenge the status quo or to persuade others. (PT, UT, CT)	3a. What is the author's purpose in writing the story? (F) 3b. How do the actions of characters or people provoke discussion? (C) 3c. What are the dynamics of productive discussions? (F) 3d. What needs to happen to move from discussion to action? (C) 3e. How does the author inspire change? (C)
4. Readers who explore multiple points of view on a topic cultivate an informed stance, which can expose and eliminate personal bias. (UT, CT, RT)	4a. What is bias? (F) 4b. How do you identify bias? (F) 4c. How do you read various viewpoints with an open mind? (P) 4d. How does reading many viewpoints support the formation of your opinion? (C) 4e. When you construct your text, how do you consider points of view? (C)
5. Writers construct and format a persuasive argument based on purpose and knowledge of the audience. (PT, UT)	5a. How do you select a topic that you are passionate about? (F) 5b. How does your choice of format/genre promote your issue? (F) 5d. How do you choose an appropriate voice for your audience and purpose? (F) 5e. What format is most effective for your particular audience? (F) 5f. What are the different text media? (F)
6. Through social action people may move others to accomplish a social imperative. (UT, RT, PT)	6a. What was the social problem in the story of _____? (F) 6b. What motivated _____ to take action? (F) 6c. Why was _____ willing to face the resistance encountered in order to achieve change? (F) 6d. When is social action not the best way to effect change? (P) 6e. Do we need social activists in the world? (P)

Key (Expected Performance):

PT: Producing Text   UT: Understanding Text   CT: Critiquing Text   RT: Responding to Text

Critical Content and Key Skills

Critical Content	Key Skills
Understanding Text: • Author's purpose in writing • Literary techniques writers use that convey author stance • How voice influences point of view • Meaning of cause and effect • Meaning of social change	Understanding Text: • Make inferences • Take a critical stance • Draw conclusions • Identify bias • Summarize two or more ideas • Interpret the author's point of view—i.e., is the author pro, con, or neutral? • Make connections • Make inferences when points of view are implicit
Responding to Text: • Group discussion norms • Importance of text evidence • Other points of view expand understanding	Responding to Text: • Use background knowledge to support an idea • Discuss characters' behaviors, relationships, attitudes, motivations • Differentiate between fact and opinion • Cite text evidence to support interpretation • Listen to what others have to say
Critiquing Text: • Author credentials • What bias means • Meaning of critical stance	Critiquing Text: • Make judgments • Compare and contrast text media • Compare/contrast multiple points of view • Take a critical stance based on fact and opinion • Identify social action issues within text • Analyze the relationships among ideas and characters
Producing Text: • Voice in writing • Persuasive letter writing • Format appropriate to audience	Producing Text: • Discern relevant information from irrelevant information • Utilize organizational strategies (hook, transitions, sentence fluency) • Use appropriate conventions, word choice, and voice • Cite sources accurately • Investigate and collect information on their topic • Integrate facts into their writing • Choose structure/genre appropriate to purpose • Use persuasive techniques to get a point across

Grade Level: 6
How Can We Change the World?

Suggested Timeline	Suggested Learning Experiences (The teacher may . . .)	Assessments [Suggested and Required (**)]	Differentiation (For Support and Extension)	Resources
Weeks 1–2	Use an anticipatory guide to launch a discussion about social action. This should be revisited at the end of the unit to compare beliefs. Brainstorm definition of social action. EU#1 Survey classes to identify issues or topics of concern/interest. Read aloud from selected picture books and/or current letters to the editor to give students exposure to social action issues. EU#1 Create a chart/discuss what social action is or is not based on short text read in class. EU#1 Have students create and present Word Wall social action vocabulary posters. EU#3 Utilize bulletin board and display student work. Review elements of nonfiction and text structure. EU#3, #5, #6	Quickwrites (**) Students self-select one of the statements from the anticipatory guide that they feel personally strong about. Students respond to Quickwrite chosen (written response). Students need to define social change. Students share their response in a whole class/small group/partner discussion. (**) Students identify and write an anticipatory statement about which they feel strongly.** Students present Word Wall word posters.**	Modeling good Quickwrite responses. Students may need to work 1:1 or in a small group to clarify ideas. Display exemplary Word Wall posters. Rephrase questions. Share models of former students' work.	Picture Books: Martin's Big Words Rosa Parks The Great Kapok Tree I Have a Dream The Other Side When Marian Sang Carl the Complainer The Story of Ruby Bridges Virgie Goes to School With Us Boys The Ballot Box Battle Ryan and Jimmy and the Well in Africa That Brought Them Together Letters to the editor from current newspapers 50 Simple Things Kids Can Do to Save the Earth Book discussion groups on student-selected novels: • The Outcasts of 19 Schuyler Place by E. L. Konigsburg • Riding the Flume by Patricia Curtis Pfitsch (T) • Hoot by Carl Hiaasen (T) • Flush by Carl Hiaasen (T) • Edwina Victorious by Susan Bonners (E) • Counting on Grace by Elizabeth Winthrop (T) • Iqbal by Francesco D'Adamo (T) • The Missing 'Gator of Gumbo Limbo * by Jean C. George (T) • A Day for Vincent Chin and Me by Jacqueline Turner Banks (T) • Stuffed by Eric Walters (E) • Lostman's River * by Cynthia DeFelice (C) The Boy Who Saved Baseball by John H. Ritter (T) * No longer in print

Key Resources:

E: Easy
T: Typical for this time of year
C: Challenging
MT: Mentor text

Note: EU means Enduring Understanding, which is another term for Generalization.

Weeks 3–6	**Introduce** the texts students will choose and arrange students into cooperative reading discussion groups. As they read, ask students to identify social action issues within their texts. EU#2 Have students **respond to literature** using the focus questions. Students meet regularly in groups to discuss focus questions: partners, small group, jigsaw, fishbowl, large group. Instruct how to format a business letter. Identify an audience (mini-lesson). Revisit/add to survey issues list created in Week 1 as anchor chart.	Exit slips. Response to literature using focus questions. Post-it note collection.	Rephrasing questions. Modeling good answers. Extra book for home use. The Boy Who Saved Baseball ON TAPE. 1:1 Reading. SPED/teacher conference for planning novel reading. Leveled books.	* Any other selections the teacher thinks are appropriate. Some suggestions are: • Windows • The Royal Bee by Frances Park and Ginger Park • Cracking the Wall: The Struggles of the Little Rock Nine by Eileen Lucas and Mark Anthony Media specialist in conjunction with teacher prepares a database of Internet resources using the brainstorm list of the students' interests. Editorials (mentor texts).
Weeks 5–6	Model: Class writes a letter to student council for _____.			
Weeks 7–8	Through brainstorming, have students identify social action issues in the world. Read various texts to show how collecting data can be used to support a specific issue. EU#1, #5 Model how to use a T-chart illustrating pros	Graphic organizer/T-chart for research collection.** Whole class/small group discussions. Persuasive paper graphic organizer.** Students will complete a rough draft.**	Modeling good answers. Rephrasing questions. Websites identified for student research to find data and information to support their argument.	Prior student work for models. Six-trait references/rubrics. Note to Teacher: The purpose of this task is to assess enduring understandings #2 and #5: Ideas in text can evoke provocative discussions that move groups to action and result in transformative change. Writers construct and format text based on knowledge of the audience they want to persuade and their purpose.

and cons around an identified issue. EU#4 Introduce the three modes of persuasive writing: all one-sided (lower), one-sided with opposing view (basic), and two-sided (upper). EU#2, #3, #5 Model how to research an issue of concern/interest, including how to use quotes from research and how to summarize nonfiction. EU#4 Teach elements of a persuasive letter. EU#2, #3, #5, #6 Various student-teacher conferences as needed. Review six-traits assessment list. Remind students of their role as peer editors and the importance of positive, constructive criticism. Have students present final drafts to small group, partner, or whole class.	Persuasive Writing via letter. Peer edit. Final persuasive piece.**	"Universal reader" utilized for text: speech assistance. Student choice for writing topic and style format of essay. Use of graphic organizers: web, flowchart, etc. Teacher-assisted note taking through dictation from students. Persuasive writing assessment list including the six traits and three modes: one-sided (lower), one-sided with opposing view (basic), and two-sided (upper). Letter formats	<u>Olivia's Birds</u> by Olivia Bouler

How Can We Change the World?

Performance Task for Social Action Unit
Letter

What: Students will investigate an issue or a concern and write a persuasive piece to convince others of its importance . . .

Why: . . . in order to understand that writers construct and format text based on purpose and knowledge of the audience, and through social action, people may move others to accomplish a social imperative.

How:

Background: You have identified what it means to take a stand and the importance of summarizing key facts and opinions of others to support a persuasive argument. You have learned the format for persuasive writing, have practiced making T-charts listing the pros and cons of an issue, and have analyzed how voice conveys an author's stance. Now you will be putting these techniques together to write a persuasive piece regarding an issue or a concern you feel passionate about.

Task: Write a persuasive letter for the local newspaper. In your piece, pose a controversial question that will provoke strong discussion with your audience and generate a desire for social action.

Audience: Readers of the local newspaper and those who would be able to support your cause.

Procedure:

1. Research your social action topic.
2. Complete a T-chart, identifying the pros and cons.
3. Form your opinion.
4. Identify your audience.
5. Write a brief summary of the pertinent information that you will use to advance your opinion.
6. Complete a graphic organizer in preparation for your rough draft.
7. Write a rough draft of a letter or editorial.
8. Edit.
9. Revise.
10. Review for facts and opinions, being sure to have a strong argument for both.
11. Final revisions.
12. Self-assess your writing.
13. Write an explanation of specific words and facts, formatting choices, and so on that you used to generate strong reactions from readers (craft report).

Writing Rubric

Name: _____ Period: _____ Teacher: _____ Date: _____

Unit End Task Writing Assignment: How Can We Change the World? Persuasive Letter

	4 — Meets Assignment Expectations With Excellence 4 = 95*	3 — Meets Assignment Expectations Satisfactorily 3 = 85	2 — Nears Assignment Expectations— Developing Understanding 2 = 75	1 — Below Assignment Expectations— Understanding Not Demonstrated 1 = 65
	*A score of 4.5 = 100 will be awarded for performance that exceeds assignment expectations in any category.			
Ideas	• Insightful and in-depth main idea, theme, or story line. • Clear, focused, and compelling. • Rich details capture audience.	• Strong main idea, theme, or story line. • Clear and focused throughout. • Details support the main ideas.	• Identifiable main idea, theme, or story line. • Not always clear to the reader. • Some great details, mixed with some generalities.	• Questionable main idea. • Fuzzy, rambling, and confusing. • Lacking details.

IDEAS:
- Position is clearly stated.
- Relevant facts are included to persuade the reader.
- Opposing argument is acknowledged in order to make the writer's position stronger.

	4	3	2	1
Organization	• Guiding map-like structure. • Varied and satisfying use of transitions. • Well-crafted hook/lead. • Thought-provoking "Go Beyond"/"So What?"	• Orderly structure. • Purposeful use of transitions. • Strong hook/lead. • Appropriate "Go Beyond"/"So What?"	• Unclear structure. • Inconsistent use of transitions. • Basic hook/lead and conclusion.	• Structure is not evident. • Little to no use of transitions. • Weak or lacking hook/lead and conclusion.

ORGANIZATION:
- Most persuasive reason is strategically placed.
- Conclusion makes the reader want to take action.

	4	3	2	1
Voice	• Thoughts and feelings are passionate and compelling. • Tone enhances meaning.	• Thoughts and feelings are engaging and expressive. • Appropriate tone for topic, audience, and purpose.	• Thoughts and feelings show some strong moments. • Acceptable tone for the topic, audience, and purpose.	• Thoughts and feelings are flat, missing, or inappropriate. • Lacks concern for audience or topic.

VOICE:

Writing Rubric

	4 Meets Assignment Expectations With Excellence 4 = 95* * A score of 4.5 = 100 will be awarded for performance that exceeds assignment expectations in any category.	3 Meets Assignment Expectations Satisfactorily 3 = 85	2 Nears Assignment Expectations—Developing Understanding 2 = 75	1 Below Assignment Expectations—Understanding Not Demonstrated 1 = 65
Word Choice	• Consistently considers audience and purpose. • Deliberate, precise, natural, vivid, and meaningful. • Creative and expressive use of language and literary techniques. **WORD CHOICE:** • Choice of words persuades the audience. • Vocabulary relevant to the topic is included. • Research is paraphrased or quoted directly and cited.	• Considers audience and purpose. • Logical and enhances meaning. • Effective use of language and literary techniques.	• Sometimes inappropriate for audience and purpose. • Sometimes effective use of language and literary techniques; may be vague, flat, or overdone (thesaurus overload).	• No consideration for audience. • Repetitious. • Ineffective use of language and literary techniques; vague, flat, or overdone (thesaurus overload).
Sentence Fluency	• Purposefully crafted length and structure to enhance the meaning. • Flows smoothly and naturally. **SENTENCE FLUENCY:**	• Varied length and structure. • Highly readable.	• Some variation in length and structure. • Some repetition or awkward moments.	• Repetitive length and structure. • Awkward, hard to read, may include run-on sentences and/or fragments.
Conventions	• Near flawless use of taught conventions: grammar and spelling, punctuation and capitalization. • Purposeful punctuation enhances meaning. **CONVENTIONS:** • Business letter format. • Citation rules. • Punctuation rules for direct quotations.	• Few minor errors in taught conventions: grammar and spelling, punctuation and capitalization. • Some purposeful punctuation enhances meaning.	• Some punctuation and capitalization errors that do not disrupt fluency. • Some grammar and spelling errors that do not interfere with meaning.	• Many convention errors prohibit effective communication of ideas.
Workshop Process	I carefully craft, fine-tune, and adjust my writing throughout the process, utilizing mini-lessons, personal reflection, and feedback from teacher/peer conferences.	I adjust my writing throughout the process, utilizing mini-lessons, personal reflection, and feedback from teacher/peer conferences.	I revise my piece some throughout the process, considering mini-lessons and feedback from teacher/peer conferences.	I pay little attention to suggestions from teacher/peer conferences to help me revise my piece.
	WORKSHOP PROCESS: *For student's self-assessment only*			

Source: Pomperaug Regional School District 15, Middlebury/Southbury, CT

(Continued)

Sixth graders are extremely enthusiastic about this unit as they learn about how others have attempted to make the world a better place and then identify a cause on which they take a stand. I have walked through classrooms implementing this unit, and the students' motivation, thinking, and focus are so high they barely notice visitors in the room. Listening in on students' conversations, you hear concepts and understandings being passionately debated. When observing their work, you see the skills and processes they are learning being applied in a context that is relevant and owned by them. The teachers in these classrooms have created a learning environment that represents "all that education should be." You will notice that many of the suggested learning experiences address multiple unit generalizations (*enduring understandings* is the term these teachers adopted). This is an excellent way for instruction to capitalize on the reciprocity among the various processes of English language arts. This unit is also implemented through a workshop framework so that there are numerous opportunities for whole group, small group, and individualized instruction in addition to student dialogue, choices in texts, and task collaboration. Take special note of the culminating assessment for the unit. The "craft report" that students write at the end of their task forces them to go back and reflect on the choices they made in writing and to make their thinking visible through an explanation. This makes sure that the task didn't fall short of the generalization being assessed. Too often, we fall into the "pothole" discussed in Chapter 8 where the assessment design never quite reaches the point of making sure we assess students' conceptual *understanding* of the "what" and "why" represented by their assigned work.

A SAMPLE HIGH SCHOOL
ENGLISH LANGUAGE ARTS UNIT

Finally, we move to a sample high school unit. This example, shown in Figure 9.3, comes from Newtown High School in Newtown, Connecticut. The importance of a unit like this cannot be overstated given the vast amount of information and misinformation in the world today.

Who wouldn't react to the thought of being manipulated? The teachers designing this unit have used a conceptual idea to pique students' interests while they are learning some critical concepts and processes in this unit. The guiding questions are closely aligned to the generalizations, incrementally guide students' thinking toward the generalization, and are varied across different question types. The key skills show the Common Core State Standards expected to be mastered by the end of this unit. You

(Text continued on page 140)

Figure 9.3 Sample High School Concept-Based English Language Arts Unit

K–12 English Language Arts Curriculum

Grade: 9

Title: Searching for the Fountain of Truth

Grade Level: 9

Unit Title: **Searching for the Fountain of Truth**

Conceptual Lens: **Bias/Truth**

Understanding Text:
- Facts versus perception
- Personal bias/motivation of people
- Persuasive techniques
- Word choice
- Attitudes, beliefs, and values
- Culture, time, and social context
- Language
- Manipulation

Responding to Text:
- Personal bias
- Reactions of others
- Influence of visual rhetoric
- Personal reflection

Unit Title:

Searching for the Fountain of Truth

Producing Text:
- Best course of action
- Response to untruths/ misrepresentation
- Persuasive essay
- Visual rhetoric
- Research-based product
- Revision process
- Writing conventions
- Audience

Critiquing Text:
- Credibility of source
- Author's bias
- Analysis of media techniques
- Effectiveness of persuasive technique

Grade Level: 9

Unit Title: **Searching for the Fountain of Truth**

Conceptual Lens: **Bias/Truth**

Unit Overview: (an engaging summary to introduce students to the unit work)

How do we know who to believe? What makes one text more believable than another? When does a tool of persuasion become a tool of manipulation? In this unit we will explore the idea that all texts attempt to manipulate us through distinct techniques. As we become more aware of the techniques, we become less susceptible to manipulation, and better at using those techniques to manipulate others, whether it be through words or images.

Connecticut Common Core State Standards addressed in this unit:

CCSS standards are referenced in the key skills section of this unit.

Grade Level: 9
Unit Title: Searching for the Fountain of Truth

Generalizations	Guiding Questions (F = factual; C = conceptual; P = provocative)
1. Authors purposefully manipulate components of the text to control audience.	1a. Why would an author want to manipulate readers' perception? (P) 1b. How does a reader guard against being manipulated? (C) 1c. What persuasive techniques does the author of the text ___ use? (F) 1d. How does an author's bias affect meaning? (C) 1e. What is the difference between a reliable and an unreliable source? (F) 1f. How do people evaluate the relevance and reliability of sources? (F) 1g. Why do authors manipulate writing conventions? (P)
2. Social context and voices of authority often disseminate bias.	2a. What is the definition of bias? (F) 2b. How does thinking on a topic change over time? (C) 2c. How do social mores lead to bias? (C) 2d. What makes someone an authority? (C)
3. Medium suggests effective persuasive techniques.	3a. What is the definition of persuasion? (F) 3b. What are techniques of persuasion? (F) 3c. How do persuasive techniques translate to different media?(C) 3d. What are effective structures for argument? (F)
4. Discourse enables participants to deepen and revise original thought.	4a. What role does discourse have in persuasion? (F) 4b. Why is it necessary to revise thinking? (C) 4c. What effect does preparedness for a discussion have on others in the group? (F) 4d. How does the setting, the time frame, and individual behavior in collegial discussions inhibit or enhance the experience? (C)
5. Authors display credibility through ethical choices.	5a. What is an ethical choice? (F) 5b. What effect do the author's choices have on his/her credibility?(C) 5c. Is it fair/ethical to use an unreliable voice/source? (P)
6. Deep text analysis may uncover reader and author bias.	6a. How does personal bias control response? (C) 6b. How does one become self-aware? (C) 6c. How does personal bias impact our understanding and choices? (C) 6d. Why should one be concerned about author bias? (C) 6e. Who has a greater responsibility in managing bias, the reader or the writer? (P)
7. Revision process, including adhering to writing and speaking conventions, strengthens the message.	7a. Why is revision important? (C) 7b. How does seeking a reader's response help writing improve? (C) 7c. Is there always a need to revise? (P)
8. Reconciling prior and new perspectives enhances one's understanding.	8a. What is sacrificed with new insight? (P) 8b. How can prior perspectives inhibit understanding something new? (C) 8c. How can a limited background perpetuate misunderstanding and create opportunity for greater manipulation? (C)

Critical Content and Key Skills

Critical Content What students will know . . .	Key Skills What students will be able to do . . .
Understanding Text: What bias is and how it influences readers Persuasive techniques (testimonial, bandwagon, statistical, plain folks, loaded words, bait and switch, glittering generalities, humor) The difference between denotation and connotation and how authors shape message through word choice Lenses that color meaning (attitudes, beliefs, values, culture, time, and social context) The role of inference	Understanding Text: RI.9–10.2. Determine a central idea of a text and analyze its development over the course of the text, including how it emerges and is shaped and refined by specific details. RI.9–10.4. Determine the meaning of words and phrases as they are used in a text, including figurative, connotative, and technical meanings; analyze the cumulative impact of specific word choices on meaning and tone (e.g., how the language of a court opinion differs from that of a newspaper).
Responding to Text Strategies for responding to texts (Post-it notes, viewing log, etc.) Visual rhetoric Personal bias	Responding to Text: W.9–10.2. Respond to precise language and domain-specific vocabulary to manage the complexity of the topic. W(HST).9–10.2.a. Introduce a topic and organize ideas, concepts, and information to make important connections and distinctions; include formatting (e.g., headings), graphics (e.g., figures, tables), and multimedia when useful to aiding comprehension. W.9–10.1.c. Use words, phrases, and clauses to link the major sections of the text, create cohesion, and clarify the relationships between claim(s) and reasons, between reasons and evidence, and between claim(s) and counterclaims.
Critiquing Text: What makes a valid source How persuasive techniques impact effectiveness of the purpose Organizational strategies Point of view Rhetoric (ethos, pathos, logos, word choice, syntax, sentence variety, organization)	Critiquing Text: RI.9–10.3. Analyze how the author unfolds an analysis or series of ideas or events, including the order in which the points are made, how they are introduced and developed, and the connections that are drawn between them. RI.9–10.2. Determine a central idea of a text and analyze its development over the course of the text, including how it emerges and is shaped and refined by specific details; provide an objective summary of the text. RI.9–10.5. Analyze in detail how an author's ideas or claims are developed and refined by particular sentences, paragraphs, or larger portions of a text (e.g., a section or chapter). RI.9–10.6. Determine an author's point of view or purpose in a text and analyze how an author uses rhetoric to advance that point of view or purpose.

	RI.9–10.7. Analyze various accounts of a subject told in different mediums (e.g., a person's life story in both print and multimedia), determining which details are emphasized in each account.
	RL.9–10.6. Analyze a particular point of view or cultural experience reflected in a work of literature.
Producing Text: The discrete stages of the writing∕ revision process How rhetoric builds a logical argument The most effective organization pattern for selected purpose The meaning of claim and counterclaims What is relevant and sufficient evidence to support and develop claims	Producing Text: **RI.9–10.1. Cite strong and thorough textual evidence to support analysis of what the text says explicitly as well as inferences drawn from the text.** **RI.9–10.8. Delineate and evaluate the argument and specific claims in a text, assessing whether the reasoning is valid and the evidence is relevant and sufficient; identify false statements and fallacious reasoning.** **RI.9–10.2. Determine a central idea of a text and analyze its development over the course of the text, including how it emerges and is shaped and refined by specific details; provide an objective summary of the text.** **RL.9–10.7. Analyze the representation of a subject or a key scene in two different artistic mediums, including what is emphasized or absent in each treatment (e.g., Auden's "Musée des Beaux Arts" and Breughel's Landscape with the Fall of Icarus).** **W.9–10.1. Write arguments to support claims in an analysis of substantive topics or texts, using valid reasoning and relevant and sufficient evidence.** ● Introduce precise claim(s), distinguish the claim(s) from alternate or opposing claims, and create an organization that establishes clear relationships among claim(s), counterclaims, reasons, and evidence. ● Develop claim(s) and counterclaims fairly, supplying evidence for each while pointing out the strengths and limitations of both in a manner that anticipates the audience's knowledge level and concerns. ● Provide a concluding statement or section that follows from and supports the argument presented. **W.9–10.4. Produce clear and coherent writing in which the development, organization, and style are appropriate to task, purpose, and audience.** **W.9–10.5. Develop and strengthen writing as needed by planning, revising, editing, rewriting, or trying a new approach, focusing on addressing what is most significant for a specific purpose and audience.**

Culminating Performance Task

WHAT? Students will investigate how bias affects truth . . .

WHY? . . . in order to understand that authors purposefully manipulate components of the text to control audience.

HOW?
Revisit the texts we examined as examples of persuasion.
Evaluate the persuasive effectiveness of those pieces.
Synthesize the strategies authors used to control audience, and create an original persuasive piece of your own using those techniques.
Analyze in writing how you used specific strategies in your piece and the effect you expect they will have on your audience.

Authors: Kathy Swift, Cathy Sosnowski, and Abigail Marks, Newtown High School
Source: Newtown Public Schools, Newtown, CT

(Continued)

will notice that much of the critical content and generalizations also support and bring relevance to the identified standards. These teachers meet regularly as an English department, so instruction can be collaboratively planned to ensure that by the end of the unit, lessons have addressed all of the unit's generalizations, critical content, and key skills.

SUMMARY

We know the importance of teacher modeling to accelerate student learning (Lanning, 2009). Specific, concrete examples also play an essential role in supporting learning and understanding. For example, in Chapter 2, this book introduced concept-based curriculum in English language arts by painting a picture of the end result—a classroom implementing concept-based curriculum—as an example of what this curriculum design is striving for in practice. Various examples of the separate components of a concept-based unit in English language arts were then inserted in subsequent chapters as models. We learn a great deal by studying examples for a variety of reasons. Examples serve as springboards to thinking, they can help confirm that our work is correct or incorrect, and they help relieve some of the mental load that comes with assimilating new knowledge.

When educators are willing to share their work, our professional community is strengthened. Not that sharing is always an easy thing to do! We all worry that our work needs to be "perfect" if it is going to go public and be scrutinized and held up as an example. Perfection is never the case with writing curriculum. It doesn't matter how many times we review and edit curriculum work; it is never "done." Units we thought were "beautiful" at the end of one work session are frequently revisited with exclamations: "What were we thinking?" "How could we have missed that?"

This is all part of the messy process of curriculum writing, so I applaud and sincerely thank those professionals who stepped out and volunteered unit examples knowing that they will be a tremendous help to others who are novices in concept-based English language arts. Practice plays a role in developing one's expertise, but with examples to support deeper understanding comes increased quality across the entire concept-based writing process. I commend you who venture forth on a quest to create "thinking cultures" in your classrooms for your adventuresome spirit. I encourage you to share your work with others and continue to refine your craft through reflection and collaboration.

10 Voices From the Field

Educators are faced with many curriculum choices. Making the decision to adopt a concept-based design to help students meet standards, whether the Common Core State Standards for English Language Arts or any other, should be a question considered by all stakeholders engaged in a language arts curriculum revision or renewal process. I believe that, when done well, concept-based curriculum and instruction ultimately chart a path toward highly positive student performance results and increased professional satisfaction for teachers. Voices of those who have experienced the process of writing and implementing a concept-based curriculum in English language arts provide the best last words for this book. In this chapter, you will hear from a superintendent, several principals, an English Department chair, an eighth-grade teacher, and an elementary language arts consultant who have done this hard work.

We begin with a collaborative reflection from a superintendent from Connecticut's North Haven Public Schools, Robert Cronin, a leader who genuinely holds curriculum and instruction as core values, and one of his principals, Mary Federico. Mary is an exemplary principal from Montowese Elementary School, who worked shoulder to shoulder with the district literacy leaders learning about concept-based curriculum. I asked both to reflect on why their district committed to writing a concept-based English language arts curriculum. Here is what they had to say:

> Our district is committed to the continuous improvement of student achievement for all students. We've approached this undertaking in a few critical ways. Recognizing the importance of consistency across grade levels, we wanted to design a curriculum specifically for a K–12 system. To be truly effective, there
>
> *(Continued)*

(Continued)

can be no "silos of practice." Therefore, a concept-based curriculum best matches our philosophy.

The district's administrative council has spent the past five months reading and discussing the book *How People Learn.* The idea of a concept-based curriculum operationalizes many of the ideas we've read about and discussed. It provides us with a way to focus teaching and learning such that we are confident we are addressing, through each unit of study and daily lesson, the ever-increasing standards all students are expected to know and be able to do at every grade level.

As we set out to develop a new K–5 language arts curriculum, the district's 10 literacy leaders, representing the four elementary schools, the middle school, and the high school, received four full days of professional development designed to assist them in establishing a shared understanding of the philosophy of a concept-based curriculum. Throughout this four-day training our group became more cohesive and began to embrace these concepts. This was the beginning of building leadership skills within this group so that people truly began to see themselves as "literacy leaders" in the district rather than reading teachers. The participants met together as a group after the training and began to strategize how to build the capacity to "buy in" at each grade level. They carefully chose classroom teachers representing kindergarten through Grade 5 from each school. The chosen teachers spent two full days of training in learning about a concept-based curriculum with our "literacy leaders" guiding them through the learning. The plan was for these teachers to meet one full day each month to begin writing the unit of study for their grade level using a common template and applying the concept-based concepts they learned about to the new curriculum document.

The elementary teachers in our district are excited about having a language arts curriculum to guide their teaching, which will align to the English language arts Common Core State Standards using a readers' workshop model. We want to show teachers that a comprehensive English language arts curriculum will take time. This type of curriculum writing is a major shift in thinking for our staff. We are carefully drafting a rollout plan with major milestones and a suggested time frame. This year our goal is to write one unit of study for each grade, K–5. Next year, each grade will pilot this one unit of study, and the district will offer professional development to all teachers on the philosophy of a concept-based curriculum, on how to incorporate a reading workshop model into their classroom practices, and on how to effectively teach

> We want to show teachers that a comprehensive English language arts curriculum will take time. This type of curriculum writing is a major shift in thinking for our staff.

writing. During the pilot year we will be making adjustments and modifications to the curriculum to promote a deep understanding of concepts and make certain there are supports in place for our teachers as they implement the language arts unit of study.

As the elementary principal who has been chosen to work with this group of teachers, I believe we are going in the right direction to move our district forward in creating a curriculum document that will improve student performance and help them become critical thinkers. I feel very positive about this work, especially having observed our teachers embracing this way of writing curriculum.

We believe that a concept-based curriculum holds tremendous promise for our students. Not only does it allow them to examine concepts and ideas in greater depth, we also believe it is exactly what we need to best provide them with the necessary 21st century skills for success both in and outside of school. Based on everything we've learned, concept-based curriculum will result in the kind of improved student achievement we are seeking.

The next reflection is from Cathy Sosnowski, the English Department chair at Newtown High School in Newtown, Connecticut. The first time I met Cathy, I knew immediately that she was a conceptual thinker with a strong background in writing curriculum. She clearly has expertise in her discipline and has a mind that is in full throttle all the time. Her succinct summary of learning about concept-based curriculum in English language arts speaks volumes.

Driving home from the training each day, I'd take concept-based learning and think about how it fit in with what I know about curriculum. While a similar model of curriculum design was good because my students could focus on essential questions, it often left me at a loss of how to address skills and concepts. As a young teacher, I'm embarrassed to admit, I just didn't address them. We were all broad brush and no detail. My kids could think; they lacked solid skills, but they could think.

Strictly using standards as outlined by another writer, I moved in a different direction. My concepts and skills were well articulated, and I was able to measure them. They were my focus. Thinking in larger terms, wrestling with essential questions got lost in the data I generated. My kids had measurably improved on the skills we prioritized; the ability to think and support that thinking was not as strong.

(Continued)

(Continued)

Like an academic Goldilocks I moved from the too broad of one design to the too narrow of another. With concept-based curriculum I may have found the "just right" spot. It allows me to go deeper and promote critical and independent thinking around a central generalization while still being mindful that the road to that generalization is built with specific processes and skills.

English language arts is a difficult match as it is not a sequential discipline such as math or science. Reading, writing, speaking, listening, and language happen concurrently, which is the most significant aspect of English language arts' outlier nature. That did make choosing a starting point to design the unit the largest stumbling block for me. By considering what skills and concepts needed to be addressed (looking at the Common Core State Standards), it helped me to maximize the power of concept-based curriculum in English language arts.

> Like an academic Goldilocks I moved from the too broad of one design to the too narrow of another. With concept-based curriculum I may have found the "just right" spot.

Mary Blair, an elementary language arts consultant also from Newtown Public Schools, shares her experience in writing concept-based curriculum. Mary is one of the most industrious and thoughtful teachers I have ever met. Her story provides honest insights into what it takes to step back from what is comfortable and familiar to considering the possibilities of something new:

When I walked into my first of three days of professional development surrounding concept-based units of study in language arts, I had no idea what to expect. I had heard of units of study, but thought immediately of content-area learning, not language arts. As I sat down with my fellow elementary language arts consultants and district colleagues and flipped open my laptop, I soon learned that I was about to embark on one of the most enlightening and challenging curriculum projects I had ever been involved in.

Traditionally, in Newtown, we have had curriculum maps built on Connecticut state standards, with a scope and sequence for each month of the year. Each individual elementary school has had the liberty to address these standards and objectives in any way seen fit using whatever authors, texts, and resources the schools wanted. Many of these overlapped across the four elementary schools in the district, but not always. To think about our curriculum in a concept-based way was extremely different, allowing for more depth of knowledge and ensuring the connection between reading and writing.

Recently there has been a push for the alignment of the four elementary schools, so concept-based units could not come at a better time. Additionally, the Common Core State Standards are providing the opportunities for districts to revamp, ramp up, and reorganize our curriculum. It is as if the stars are in alignment.

One of the things that helped us choose titles for our units of study was unpacking the units that were already being taught in each elementary school. Once we had this information, it was easy to identify redundancies and gaps and create a district map of potential units that would lend themselves to concept-based curriculum and support system-wide coherence. Thinking about the conceptual lenses for the units was a whole other story. Even months later, we have made changes to our lenses and even the titles of our units. The units themselves, however, have remained constant. There has also been conversation with the middle and high school teachers to ensure that the units build from year to year. We all need to support one another in making sure that our students leave high school with the skills they need to compete in today's fast-paced world.

The initial stage of learning about concepts, generalizations, focus questions, and conceptual lenses was quite overwhelming. Thinking about curriculum in this three-dimensional manner requires thinking about the knowledge and complex processes we want students to learn and be able to transfer from one situation and discipline to another. The format of concept-based units is also much different. The format is more detailed and concise. The units are, however, easy, even for new teachers, to understand and implement because all of the curriculum expectations and resources are in the same place.

> One of the things that helped us choose titles for our units of study was unpacking the units that were already being taught in each elementary school.

Among other things, our group struggled with writing the generalizations and focus questions. The wording of these statements and questions must be precise. We often had to write and rewrite multiple times. Writing this part of the unit has been the most time consuming but also the most rewarding in terms of professional conversations. We want to make sure that the generalizations are rigorous enough and that the focus questions guide students toward what we want them to learn.

> The units are easy, even for new teachers, to understand and implement because all of the curriculum expectations and resources are in the same place.

Perhaps the greatest challenge we now face is finding the time to complete the units and train other teachers and, finally, develop a plan for rollout. Our

(Continued)

(Continued)

plan is for the elementary language arts consultants to complete a large portion of the units and to involve teachers when the lesson planning sections are to be completed. We have yet to find time to continue our work that we started during the five professional development days we had. We are determined not to let this important work fall by the wayside. Too much time and energy has already been put forth. I look forward to continuing the work to lift the thinking level of not only student knowledge but also professional knowledge.

Deborah Schultz's thoughts are next. Deborah has a unique perspective to offer because she was an eighth-grade middle school English language arts teacher when she was first introduced to concept-based curriculum. She is now an assistant principal in the same building, continuing to champion the effort of concept-based curriculum and instruction. You can "hear" how she initially struggled. As a long-standing teacher with a reputation for procuring high student performance, she was not convinced that concept-based curriculum would work in English, but she was transformed as her understanding deepened.

I was first introduced to concept-based curriculum and instruction when Lynn Erickson came to Region 15 and led our opening two-day professional development activity. At the time I was the language arts coordinator for Rochambeau Middle School, and was teaching seventh- and eighth-grade English.

While the concept and application of this new type of curriculum writing was easily understood for the disciplines of history and science, I had great difficulty in "wrapping my brain around it" and making it work for English. Feeling stupid (and knowing I wasn't), I asked my principal for additional training, and she, a technical education teacher, and I traveled to Boston to attend another workshop being given by Lynn. I remained unable to "make it work" for the discipline of English.

I reached the conclusion that this was because the other disciplines taught identifiable "nouns"—systems, organisms, cycles, environment, earth, transportation, civilization, economics, geography, government—whereas English teachers teach "verbs"—reading and writing. Whenever we attempted to write a concept for English, we ended up focusing on the skills of reading and writing.

The other impediment we faced was the fact that we were teaching "books," or core novels, throughout our English curriculum.

Seventh grade taught *The Witch of Blackbird Pond*, *My Brother Sam Is Dead*, *The Outsiders*, and *The High King*.

Eighth grade taught *Night*, *The Contender*, *To Kill a Mockingbird*, and *Heroes, Gods and Monsters of the Greek Myths*.

There were no connecting concepts—no timeless, universal constructs (other than the skills [verbs] of reading and writing [interpreting, analyzing, critiquing, etc.])—that were transferrable from one novel to the next. Neither did the culminating performance tasks (often, but not always, a writing piece) connect to each other.

Then, about two years later, Gay Ivey came to our district to lead a professional development day on student choice in reading. After hearing her speak, I recognized the value of moving away from the standard of teaching one core novel to all students, regardless of interest and reading ability levels. It was this broadening and expansion of ideas that led me to reconsider whether or not a concept-based curriculum was doable in English.

My first foray into allowing choice in reading occurred in my seventh-grade English class. I alone piloted an experiment. Given the fact that two of our core novels (*The Witch of Blackbird Pond* and *My Brother Sam Is Dead*) were coordinated to parallel the seventh-grade history curriculum (early colonial life and the American Revolution), I decided to continue the theme of paralleling with the history class and have my students read books focusing on the Civil War, a unit the seventh-grade history classes were supposed to end the school year with. I coordinated with my town's public library, which loaned me every book it had (appropriate to seventh graders) focusing on the Civil War. The number totaled more than 100, and my students were allowed to browse through them all and choose one that interested them.

Instructionally speaking, I was in over my head. I now had 100 students each reading a different book based on one topic: the Civil War. Having not read any of the books, I was unfamiliar with them, and could not ask the typical teacher questions regarding them. In addition, I had asked the librarian for *all* the books (and since I had 100 students, I needed as many books), which meant that some students were reading fiction but the majority were reading nonfiction.

Not only was the district moving to a concept-based design for all curricula, but my circumstances, caused by introducing choice, forced me to begin teaching conceptually! My teacher-directed questions had to be general: What was the author's purpose in writing this book? What message did you get as the reader? What interested you most about what you read? What horrified you? What similarities/contrasts can you discuss with your neighbor?

My biggest fear was that my principal would walk into my room to do an observation and discover that I had lost total control of my classes! While I gave some direction and guidance, most of the discussion was student directed. I was never more relieved than when that experiment was finished and I could return to being in full charge of my classroom. I handed out the obligatory student survey, and waited for the hits to come. Surely the students would note that I appeared unprepared and floundering!

I was therefore totally flabbergasted at the student response: "This was the BEST unit ever!" "I LOVED being able to choose my own book!" "Can we do

(Continued)

(Continued)

more of these?" "Is this how it's going to be when we get to eighth grade? . . . I hope so," and on and on.

How could I not offer this opportunity to them again? What could I do to increase student choice of texts and support more conceptually based learning?

> My biggest fear was that my principal would walk into my room to do an observation and discover that I had lost total control of my classes!

Because I was teaching eighth grade as well, I turned my sights in that direction. For years, every eighth grader had read the memoir *Night,* by Elie Wiesel—a fabulous and deeply moving book, but not the only memoir written by a Holocaust survivor. This book also coincided with the history curriculum and the eighth-grade field trip to Washington, DC, where students visited the Holocaust Memorial Museum. The culminating writing task at the end of reading the memoir was a thesis paper, a performance task I supported as it was the students' first foray into this type of writing and a necessary "first step" to prepare them for high school. What I didn't like was the "shallowness" of the paper. Unfortunately, the thesis statement was not only contrived, but prescriptive; every single student had to use the same statement: *The title,* Night, *is a good title because . . .* A chore for both writer and reader (me!).

After securing permission from my principal for an additional "pilot," a further "experiment," I spent the summer of 2005 reading every age-appropriate Holocaust-survivor memoir I could find and settled on six different memoirs (*Night* was still included). I ordered enough books for student choice within all my classes, while securing student discussion groups numbering three to four students (one important lesson learned from the Civil War experiment!).

Prior to choosing the memoir they wanted to read, students were advised that they would be writing a thesis paper as a culminating activity and would need to cite evidence from their book to support their thesis statement. To guide students (and give them the opportunity to provide "Post-it" evidence as they read), I gave them an overarching question: *What characteristics are necessary to be a survivor?*

And so began one of the most enjoyable times of my teaching career. Students were thrilled to have the opportunity to choose their own book to read. I had a variety of reading ability levels, and had been careful to choose an equal mix of male survivors and female survivors, cognizant of the fact that while girls will happily read about males or females, boys are more interested in reading about males. Group discussions were student-directed and student-led. The "cross-talk" among the groups led to many students reading more than one memoir as they got interested in each other's survivors.

Using a picture book, *The Cats in Krasinski Square,* I taught students how to gather and cite evidence to use in their thesis paper, and the result was phenomenal. Students wrote about relationships (with family, friends, and strangers), the human condition, the depth of love (and hatred), the pull of family and implied responsibility, hope, courage, and so on and so forth.

For me, there was no going back! No more core novels, no more dragging all students through one book whether they liked it or not, and whether they were able to read it or not.

We then went from teaching a book, *Night,* to deciding we would call the new unit "The Holocaust." Two errors emerged: First it was a topic (versus a concept), and second it was a social studies topic, not a language arts focus.

Next we tried "Tolerance," a concept in literature, but not so much during the Holocaust!

Finally, we settled on the unit of study: "Humanity Versus Inhumanity: Memoirs of/from the Holocaust." The conceptual lens is critical stance.

The biggest stumbling block at this point was that the classroom teachers did not want to give up control. Teachers are most comfortable and familiar with directing instruction; concept-based curriculum requires them to give up that role. They must become the guide on the side, instead of the sage on the stage.

It was difficult to move teachers forward to this new idea, and so with some desperation, it was suggested that we begin each grade with a novel teachers were already comfortable with and could incorporate in a conceptual unit (like I had done with *Night*).

Eighth grade: *To Kill a Mockingbird* was incorporated into a coming of age/ perspectives unit.

Seventh grade: *The Witch of Blackbird Pond* and *My Brother Sam Is Dead* were incorporated into a historical fiction unit.

The Outsiders and *The High King* were incorporated into a conceptual unit on good and evil or, as it stands now, "Is Human Nature Universal?"

Sixth grade: *Hoot* was incorporated into a social change unit.

Fifth grade: *Hatchet* was incorporated into a unit on survival (particularly focusing on the conflict of man against nature).

Then began the journey of rewriting the curriculum—a difficult, but worthwhile and fulfilling, process. Concept-based curriculum goes deep beneath the surface of instruction and learning, and it is that very depth that requires commitment and intelligence from those creating it and teaching it.

I believe that the English teachers at Rochambeau Middle School had less difficulty "buying in" to concept-based curriculum because I (as a teacher and teacher leader) had "mucked around in it" myself, learned what didn't work, and fine-tuned what did. I was not an authority figure telling the teachers what they had to do; I was a practitioner who had tried it first, had revised it, and could assist them in their questions and concerns. I was also so thrilled with the student results, and so invested with this type of instruction, that my excitement was contagious.

> I believe that the English teachers at Rochambeau Middle School had less difficulty "buying in" to concept-based curriculum because I (as a teacher and teacher leader) had "mucked around in it" myself.

(Continued)

(Continued)

Our high reading scores on our state tests in sixth, seventh, and eighth grade give evidence and support for the positive results of the new curriculum.

One of the beauties of concept-based English curriculum is the ability to continually add texts to units. Two years ago, *The Hunger Games* was purchased as an additional choice in the seventh-grade unit "Is Human Nature Universal?" The phenomena of this book/series have now been evidenced on the silver screen, and have done much to turn kids on to reading.

And, finally, I present a story of success and hard work from a principal who has been providing courageous and enthusiastic leadership to ensure implementation of a concept-based curriculum across all disciplines in his building. Anthony Salutari is the principal of Rochambeau Middle School (RMS) in Southbury, Connecticut, where Deborah (above) also works. He is committed to excellence in teaching and learning and "walks the talk" by ensuring his staff members have the structures and support they need to successfully implement concept-based curriculum with fidelity.

When I first began my current role as middle school principal, many of the content-area curricula were in the revision stages. The revisions were focused on moving away from the more traditional curricula (a list of objectives) to concept-based curriculum design. This was a significant change that resulted in varied levels of stress for many teachers.

Over the past six years, I have seen a tremendous amount of progress regarding the comfort level of teachers who are now consistently employing concept-based curricula. This comfort level has led to the improved effectiveness of the delivery of instruction that has had a very positive impact on student performance. In reflecting on the past six years, I believe a few key areas are responsible for the improved instruction and student performance. For the record, my expertise in concept-based curriculum was minimal at best. With that being said, it was crucial that the staff members responsible for developing the curricula were experts in this area. This was certainly the case in Region 15. Once the quality curriculum was in place, the first step I took was to clearly communicate the expectation that all teachers follow the curriculum. Although this should be assumed, teachers sometimes teach what they want if they are not informed of specific expectations. In addition to establishing the expectation of implementing the established curriculum, I made a revision in the use of team meeting time. More specifically, three days per week, one period each day was focused on grade-level, content-area meetings. During these meetings, teachers were required to plan upcoming lessons and assessments while referencing the curriculum. Minutes of these meetings were submitted to me on a monthly basis.

Within the minutes, teachers were to identify where they were in the curriculum and explain any pacing concerns they identified. Over time, discussions during content-area meetings became more focused on the consistent delivery of the curriculum and the implementation of common assessments. This allowed teachers the opportunity to review student performance on common assessments and adjust upcoming lessons based on student needs.

At first, teachers balked at the new focus on team meeting time, but over the years, teachers have come to truly value this time that is devoted to teaching and learning. Since we follow the professional learning community model at our middle school, meeting time during the day was provided. Without providing teachers with this additional planning period, the expectation of grade-level content-area teachers consistently implementing the curriculum and using common assessments would have been far less successful. It is worth stating that this team meeting time was in addition to teachers' preparation period, not instead of it.

I made it a point to observe teachers based on the grade level and content area they teach. Any discrepancies I noticed in either the content being taught or the pacing of the teachers was brought to their attention quickly and with the expectation that there was a solid explanation why. We are lucky to have instructional teacher leaders (ITLs) in each academic area. I would share some of my observations with the ITLs, and they would make it a point to add my suggestions to their monthly meeting agendas. My observations were not designed as a "gotcha," but more designed to ensure the clearly established expectation that curriculum implementation was occurring. Getting in classrooms allowed me to recognize some of the improvements teachers were making with curriculum implementation. I also made it a point to identify in the observation write-up the specific implementation of the curriculum if it was observable. This feedback was not only well received by teachers, but was a way to reinforce my established expectation regarding the use of the curriculum. Over the past few years, I have made it a point to consistently remind faculty of the importance of using the curriculum. Since our English language arts concept-based curriculum supports increased student choice, I also worked diligently to ensure teachers had the required materials to teach the various units in their curriculum.

> Since our English language arts concept-based curriculum supports increased student choice, I worked diligently to ensure teachers had the required materials to teach the various units in their curriculum.

Professional development is a perfect opportunity to support concept-based curriculum implementation. In speaking with teachers in my building, we came to the conclusion that full faculty professional development was not always the best use of time. Over time, we have moved away from the infamous full faculty professional development and now meet by content area and grade level. During this time, teachers work directly with the curriculum as they plan upcoming lessons and assessments. Our ITLs

(Continued)

(Continued)

and our reading consultant provided support for teachers as they learned and employed the revisions to the curriculum. The ITL support, as well as the overall change to the professional development arrangement, has been especially valuable. I encourage all building-based administrators to consider this when planning professional development.

Was our transformation from more traditional curriculum to concept-based curriculum an easy one? It most certainly was not. Was it worth it? Absolutely. When I am lucky enough to get out of my office and visit classrooms, I am more and more impressed with the quality of instruction that is occurring. Students are expected to think and learn at a higher level. Instruction is focused on moving students toward *understanding* rather than recalling information. Content and material allow for choice, making learning more interesting and relevant for students. And, as mentioned earlier, our test scores have improved. For example, six years ago, the percent of students in our school reaching the goal level in reading on the state assessment hovered in the high 70% to low 80% range. Steady progress has been made, and our most recent reading scores on the state assessment, in all three grade levels, are over 90%. I am very impressed with these significant improvements and am confident our student performance will continue to improve.

> Was our transformation from more traditional curriculum to concept-based curriculum an easy one? It most certainly was not. Was it worth it? Absolutely.

Our success has been a result of quality curricula, ongoing and focused professional development, common planning time, clearly established expectations, recognition of success, and a willingness by all faculty members to make decisions that are in the best interests of our students. I am still not an expert in concept-based curriculum, but I am doing what I can to deepen my understanding as the improvements I have observed at RMS have been a direct result of the consistent implementation of our concept-based curriculum.

I am incredibly appreciative of the professionals behind these chronicles and for the scores of other teachers I have had the privilege of working with in designing concept-based curriculum. They always stretch my thinking, amaze me with their insights, and confirm my beliefs about all that is possible. They make the ideas presented in this book whole.

References

Anderson, L. W., & Krathwohl, D. R. (Eds.). (2001). *A taxonomy for learning, teaching, and assessing: A revision of Bloom's taxonomy of educational objectives.* New York: Addison Wesley Longman, Inc.

Bransford, J. D., Brown, A. L., & Cocking, R. R. (Eds.). (1999). *How people learn: Brain, mind, experience, and school.* Washington, DC: National Academies Press.

Common Core State Standards Initiative. (2010). *Common Core State Standards for English Language Arts.* Retrieved from http://www.corestandards.org/assets/CCSSI_ELA%20Standards.pdf

Erickson, H. Lynn. (2007). *Concept-based curriculum and instruction for the thinking classroom.* Thousand Oaks, CA: Corwin Press.

Erickson, H. Lynn. (2008). *Stirring the head, heart, and soul: Redefining curriculum, instruction, and concept-based learning* (3rd ed.). Thousand Oaks, CA: Corwin Press.

Glatthorn, A. A. (1987). *Curriculum renewal.* Alexandria, VA: Association for Supervision and Curriculum Development.

Harris, T., & Hodges, R. (1995). *The literacy dictionary: The vocabulary of reading and writing.* Newark, DE: International Reading Association.

Hattie, J. A. (2009). *Visible learning: A synthesis of over 800 meta-analyses relating to achievement.* New York: Routledge.

Kotter, J., & Rathgeber, H. (2005). *Our iceberg is melting: Changing and succeeding under any conditions.* New York: Saint Martin's Press.

Lanning, L. A. (2009). *Four powerful comprehension strategies for struggling readers Grades 3–8: Small group instruction that improves comprehension.* Thousand Oaks, CA: Corwin Press.

Marzano, R. J. (2003). *What works in schools: Translating research into action.* Alexandria, VA: Association for Supervision and Curriculum Development.

Newmann, F. M., Smith, B., Allensworth, E., & Bryk, A. S. (2001). Instructional program coherence: What it is and why it should guide school improvement policy. *Education Evaluation and Policy Analysis, 23*(4), 297–321.

Perkins, D. (1992). *Smart schools: Better thinking and learning for every child.* New York: Free Press.

Perkins, D. (2009). *Making learning whole.* San Francisco: Jossey-Bass.

Schmoker, M. (2011). *Focus: Elevating the essentials to radically improve student learning.* Alexandria, VA: Association for Supervision and Curriculum Development.

Shoemaker, J. E., & Lewin, L. (1993). Curriculum and assessment: Two sides of the same coin. *Educational Leadership, 50*(8), 55–57.

Sternberg, R. J. (1996). Attention and consciousness. In R. J. Sternberg (Ed.), *Cognitive psychology* (pp. 68–107). New York: Harcourt Brace.

Turner, J. (2003). *Ensuring what is tested is taught: Curriculum coherence and alignment.* Arlington, VA: Educational Research Service.

Zazkis, R., Liljedahl, P., & Chernoff, E. (2007). *The role of examples in forming and refuting generalizations.* Retrieved from http://blogs.sfu.ca/people/zazkis/wp-content/uploads/2010/05/2008-zentralblatt-didaktic.pdf

Index

CORWIN
A SAGE Company

The Corwin logo—a raven striding across an open book—represents the union of courage and learning. Corwin is committed to improving education for all learners by publishing books and other professional development resources for those serving the field of PreK–12 education. By providing practical, hands-on materials, Corwin continues to carry out the promise of its motto: **"Helping Educators Do Their Work Better."**